Managed Services Operatic

Standard Operating Procedures for Computer Consultants and Managed Service Providers

Volume Three: Running the Service Department

SOPs for Managing Technicians, Daily Operations, Service Boards, and Scheduling

Karl W. Palachuk

Published by

(G L B

Great Little Book Publishing

Sacramento, CA
www.GreatLittleBook.com

Great Little Book Publishing

Sacramento, CA

Managed Services Operations Manual: Standard Operating Procedures for Computer Consultants and Managed Service Providers

Volume Three: Running the Service Department SOPs for Managing Technicians, Daily Operations, Service Boards, and Scheduling

Copyright © 2014 by Karl W. Palachuk

All rights reserved.

Parts of this book are derived from blog posts written by Karl W. Palachuk at http://blog.smallbizthoughts.com.

ISBN 978-0-9905923-4-1 (for this volume)

ISBN 978-1-942115-05-2 (for this volume on Kindle)

ISBN 978-1-942115-01-4 (for this volume on Smashwords)

ISBN 978-0-9905923-1-0 (for the 4-volume set)

ISBN 978-0-9905923-6-5 (for the Kindle 4-volume set)

ISBN 978-0-9905923-7-2 (for the Smashwords 4-volume set)

No part of this document may be used or reproduced in any manner whatsoever without written permission.

www.greatlittlebook.com

Electronic Contents

This book includes a few additional downloads what you will find very helpful. These include Word files, and a few other goodies.

If you purchased this book from SMB Books or Great Little Book, you should have received a download link when your purchase was completed.

If you lost that or purchased from Amazon or another reseller, you can register at www.SMBBooks.com.

Please have your purchase receipt ready to register. You'll need the Order ID. If your purchase somewhere other than SMBBooks.com, you'll need to forward proof of purchase to us.

Please respect our copyright and do not make unauthorized copies of these documents.

We welcome your feedback. Please email *karlp@greatlittlebook.com*.

Warning about Used Books

When you register your book online, you agree that the book is no longer returnable for a refund. We simply have to assume that anyone who registers the book is going to download the electronic content and use it. Therefore, the book cannot be returned once the e-version has been downloaded. That also means that the owner of a used copy of the book does not have access to the electronic content. Thank you for your support and understanding.

Copyright © 2014 Karl W. Palachuk

Copyright © 2014 Karl W. Palachuk

Managed Services Operations Manual

Standard Operating Procedures for Computer Consultants and Managed Service Providers

Volume Three: Running the Service Department

SOPs for Managing Technicians, Daily Operations, Service Boards, and Scheduling

Karl W. Palachuk

Table of Contents

Copyright © 2014 Karl W. Palachuk

Copyright © 2014 Karl W. Palachuk

Copyright © 2014 Karl W. Palachuk

About The Author

Karl W. Palachuk has been an IT Consultant since 1995 and is one of the pioneers of the managed services business model. One of his books - *Managed Services in a Month* - has been the number one book on managed services on Amazon.com for more than five years.

Karl is a popular blogger among managed service providers and produces a wide variety of educational events each year, ranging from online classes, in-personal seminars, and the only all-online three-day conference in the SMB channel.

"Everything we do," says Karl, "is intended to help technology consultants be better with the business side of their business."

You can always catch up with him at www.SmallBizThoughts.com.

www.facebook.com/karlpalachuk

www.twitter.com/karlpalachuk

www.linkedin.com/in/karlpalachuk

www.pinterest.com/karlpalachuk

YouTube.com/SmallBizThoughts

www.tumblr.com/blog/smallbizthoughts

Copyright © 2014 Karl W. Palachuk

Copyright © 2014 Karl W. Palachuk

Acknowledgements

I have written or co-written eleven books before this. With this four-volume set I am publishing my 12th, 13th, 14th, and 15th books. More than any project I've ever been involved in, this set of books has been a HUGE effort and a HUGE collaborative effort.

I have over 100 people to thank for making these books possible. Some are co-workers. Some are friends. Some are business associates. And I am proud to say that some are "strangers." (Not really strangers any more since they helped with this project.)

The Story

The story of this four-volume set has three major chapters. First, I started blogging about SOPs – Standard Operating Procedures – on Fridays. I called it *SOP Friday* and even registered the domain name *SOPFriday.com*. You can still go there to get a list of blog posts in an "index" format.

Second, I put together a big fund-raising campaign at Indiegogo.com to raise money to speed up the publication process. It takes a lot of money to produce a book set like this. As a result, raising money allowed me to speed up how quickly I was able to have the money needed for design, layout, etc.

Third, I gathered up all the SOPs from the blog, plus a number that we've used in the businesses I've run over the last twenty years. I had to reorganize the contents quite a bit to make it make sense. Then I

Copyright © 2014 Karl W. Palachuk

had to fill in some gaps. I was surprised at how much writing still remained. So I got to work at that.

Thanks

Huge thanks go out to my friend Monica Caraway for helping with this project. Monica serves as my Marketing Manager and spearheaded the successful Indiegogo campaign.

And of course I thank every single person who contributed to the Indiegogo campaign. Here are those who agreed to have their names published:

Lars Andersson	David Armstrong
Daniel Ashurst	Derik T Bahl
Steven Banks	Matt Beardon
Scott Bechtold	Don Bentz
Sam Berar	Frank Boecherer
Jeff Bolden	Chris Braham
Frank Bravata	Rory Breen
Sharon Broughton	Rayanne Buchianico
Lauren Buchland	Dan Buhler
MIchael Campbell	Steve Carter
Brett Chalmers	Stephanie Chandler
Jeremy Christensen	Robin Cole
Robert C Coop	Robert Coppedge
Ross Coutts	Charles Dalton
Deal Consulting, Inc.	Ana Diaz
Ryan Dobb	Benjamin Duncan
Jonathan Elliott	Raul Espino
Bob Farkas	James Forbis
Randall Garner	David P Grinder

Copyright © 2014 Karl W. Palachuk

Thomas H Lem Jr
Jonathan Henderson
Anthony Iaccino
Jamie Jensen
Maggie Jones
Leonard Keao
Jakub Kosiec
Thomas Kragh
David Libby
Joshua D Liberman
Eric Long
Steve Marfisi
Darryl McAllister
Tom McKay
Stanley Ng Kian Meng
Bob Milliken
Simon Morley
Juan Nieves
David Okeefe
Rajendra J Patel
Sheldon Penner
Scott Phillips
Dr Gary Porter
Craig Ray
Adam Rowley
Kenneth Shafter
Dewayne Smith
Vikis Sood
Gjeret Stein
Russ Swall
Thomas Tassi
Don Tibbits

Alan Helbush
Shane Hicks
Raffi Jamgotchian
Candice Jones
Thomas Karakis
Henry Knoop
Louie Kouvelas
Hank Leander

Michael Lindsay
Nick Mancuso
James Martin
Kenneth McDermott
Shane McParland
Bob Michie
Scott Minke
Robert Nelson
Vijay Nyayapati
Manny Oliva
Sheldon Penner
Eric Penney
Duleep Pillai
Marlon N. Ramanan
Alexander Romp
Shawn Scott
Biren Shukla
Ray Smith
Clive Start
Nathan Stone
Rich Szymanski
Sean Thompson
Kevin Tobey

Copyright © 2014 Karl W. Palachuk

John Vighetto	Kevin Vinitsky
Mark Ward	Josh Weiss
Michael R West	Julian Wilkinson
John Zanazzi	Ron Zayac

. . . And Thank You to the entire SMB consulting community for your continued support over all these years.

- karlp

Karl W. Palachuk

Copyright © 2014 Karl W. Palachuk

A Note About KPEnterprises

For sixteen years I owned and operated KPEnterprises Business Consulting, which has been the model for my experiences and writing over the last decade. But people and businesses evolve.

KPEnterprises was closed down at the end of 2011 and is now simply a brand name underneath Great Little Book Publishing Co., Inc. I am spending most of my time writing, consulting, and training on the "GLB" business. The old MSP business is now owned by someone else.

I do operate a small MSP with just a few clients, called Karl Palachuk Enterprises. I do that to keep my nose in the business. It keeps me up to date on strategic planning, sales, project management, and some network migrations.

I am also a business coach. I keep five or fewer clients so that I can have time to spend on writing, blogging, traveling, etc. This mix works great for me. I get to play with new technology. I get to interact with clients. I get to keep my fingers in the support side of the business.

So . . . when I refer to KPEnterprises in this book, I am either referring to the company I owned for sixteen years or the current company I work with. They are run essentially the same.

Copyright © 2014 Karl W. Palachuk

Copyright © 2014 Karl W. Palachuk

Section I

Policies and Philosophies

Copyright © 2014 Karl W. Palachuk

Copyright © 2014 Karl W. Palachuk

1

Welcome to the Service Department

Volumes Three and Four in this book series are all about the Service Department. They are roughly divided between running the department (Volume Three) and the actual delivery of services (Volume Four).

Before we dive in, let me first pay tribute to The Service Manager. You may have a different name for this person. And, in fact, you may be the service manager. The manager of the service delivery department in any service-oriented business is the single most important person in the company.

When all the systems fall down, this person has to stand up and take charge. Every client will love him. Every client will hate him. The same is true for all employees. This person makes all the hard decisions and has to manage prima donnas at every level.

I hope he is paid very well and loves every minute of this job, because it can be amazingly reward and frustrating.

If you find a great service manager, you can build a business with no limits whatsoever. If you have a bad service manager, your company will go downhill quickly, and may never recover.

It is the service manager's job to take the last two volumes of this series and turn them into his daily operations manual. He will edit

Copyright © 2014 Karl W. Palachuk

them, mold them, shape them, and create the culture that IS your company.

> Please don't miss the implication of what I just said:

> The service manager might start with some guidelines I present here, but he must turn them into his own set of tools and resources.

At the end of the day, the service manager will be responsible for the actions of every technician. He will keep the sales people from selling something you can't deliver. He will be the one single person who makes your company profitable with his daily decisions. He will be your primary contact with clients. He will keep them happy and keep them coming back for more.

You service manager will coordinate all relationships between your departments, your employees, your vendors, your clients, and the principals of the company. (And the principles of the company, for that matter.)

Begin this process by handing these books to your service manager. But if he's good, he will fine-tune and update every single page until he has built your company into his ideal vision of what a service business can be.

Copyright © 2014 Karl W. Palachuk

2

Naming Conventions for Machines and Servers

Let's get started with the basics: machine names. Believe it or not, we have some rules around machines names. Actually, we have one super important rule, one preferred process, and a bunch of minor guidelines.

There are four sets of names you need to worry about on a regular basis: Domains, Servers, Workstations, and Printers. You might have additional devices (scanners, time clocks, nuclear imaging devices, etc.) for some clients. For all of these, the guidelines we use for printers will suffice.

Why Do We Have Names?

As silly as it sounds, people like to find machines and devices by name and not by IP address. Once you allow people to name things, they tend to choose things they like. In my file of strange and interesting bits of knowledge from the past, I have several printouts of various reports on the popularity of machine names.

It used to be easy to compile these before there was a distributed DNS system. Believe it or not, there was a time when you had to download the latest HOSTS file in order to access all the machines on the Internet. Of course that made it easy to grep the hosts file and run analyses.

Copyright © 2014 Karl W. Palachuk

A good example of this is found in *RFC 1296: Internet Growth 1981-1991* (See http://tools.ietf.org/html/rfc1296). In 1992, the most common host names were Venus, Pluto, Mars, Jupiter, Saturn. The planet theme is very clear here. Greek gods, characters from The Hobbit, Star Trek, and the Seven Dwarfs are well represented too.

But even 20 years ago, it is clear that simple workstation numbers were very popular. PC1, PC2, PC3, Mac1, Mac2, Mac3. Those series (PC and Mac) represent 28 of the 100 most common machine names.

I like themes. Just remember that one theme can simply be the machine's most basic identity (server01, workstation02, printer03, etc.). Just be prepared to take some grief if you use these labels, even though they are perfectly acceptable.

One of my favorite sources for lists of names is (Are you ready for this?) http://listofnames.info. They have text files filled with names in every category you can image, including

- Common male names
- Common female names
- Surnames
- Finnish names
- Tolkien names
- Names of actors
- Movie characters
- Shakespearean characters
- Basketball players
- . . . and more

Limitations on Names

Keep in mind that there are some common sense limitations to domain and machines names. There are limits within NetBIOS, limits within DNS, and operating system limits. You should stay within the most restrictive limits. That means you should keep machine names to 15 characters or less.

Microsoft has a history of both allowing and encouraging you to make stupid decisions about domain names and machine names. Bad decisions here WILL bite you in the butt later on down the road. For example . . .

- Since Windows 2000, 64 bit machines can have very long machine names. Don't do it.

- Older versions of SBS defaulted to renaming machines for the current user. Don't do it.

- NT 3.5 and 4.0 allowed domain with hyphens. Once active directory showed up on the scene, these machines (e.g., SBS servers) could not become domain controllers. Ouch.

- For a while (e.g., SBS 2003), Microsoft encouraged you to use your public domain name (e.g., KPEnterprises.com) as your internal domain name. This led to all kinds of problems down the road. Most people were sharp enough to use .local or some other "fake" domain extension, so they avoided problems down the road.

Lesson: Be careful about advice from Microsoft on computer names.

Also note that some operating systems deal with hyphenation better than others. So avoid it. Don't start machine names with a number. That can be confusing to some programs. Start with an alpha

Copyright © 2014 Karl W. Palachuk

character. User numbers if you want. But avoid spaces and any special characters.

The One Big Rule

I mentioned that we only have one big rule. We have already discussed it a bit:

> **Rule: Do NOT name machines after their users.**

> **Corollary: Do not name machines after their function.**

When small businesses first started getting computers, they were delighted to be able to name things. The server was named Server. Bob's machine was named Bob, Carol's machine was named Carol. And that was great for a while. Then Bob left and Ted took his place. Alice was hired and got Carol's machine as a hand-down.

So Ted's machine is named Bob. Alice's machine is named Carol. And Carol's new machine can't be named Carol because you can't have two machines with the same name.

The problem can arise if you re-purpose a server. When SQL1 is replaced with SQL2, you might want to use that old machine as a file server. So the file server is now named SQL1. Yes, you could rename it, but then you begin to create the kind of spider-webbed active directory you say you hate. Remember that renaming a machine always leaves residue. This is less of a problem than it used to be, but why take steps that "might" be troublesome down the road?

This is a pain in the neck on desktops and a minor annoyance on servers.

Copyright © 2014 Karl W. Palachuk

The One Preferred Process

I mentioned that we have one big rule (above) and one preferred process. Our preferred process is very simple. We like to name the "big" server with the date it was new. This applies primarily to small business environments. For example, our favorite server names are

- SBS2011

- SBS2010

- Johnson2012

- Unity2013

- ABC2014

The core machine name is either the client's name (Johnson, Unity, ABC), or simply SBS. The date is the year the machine was installed. It is not the server version number. Clients don't care about server versions (2003, 2008, 2011).

The date format allows you to see at a glance how old the server is. You can use this to help diagnose problems. You can also use it to remind the client of how old the server is. "Well, sir, XYZ2004 is now ten years old. Some of the slowness you're experiencing may be related to that!"

In addition, this habit allows you to quickly identify machines. If all your servers are named SBS or Server, that's not helpful. It reminds me of all the resumes we get named "resume.doc" (not helpful).

Bunch of Minor Guidelines

So, how do we recommend naming machines? Here are some miscellaneous guidelines.

First, if you can get the client to go along, try the basic Station1, Station2, Station3 or Workstation1, Workstation2, Workstation3. Yeah, I know it's boring. But it's easy and straight forward. More and more clients are accepting this. Unlike ten years ago, desktop machines are now just another part of business. They're no longer a play-thing.

Second, pick a name that includes part of the company's name and a workstation number. This is our favorite. ABC01, ABC02, ABC03, etc. It is handy if you already have a 3- or 4-digit code for each client. Just use that.

Third, if the client wants something more imaginative, have them pick a theme. Depending on the size of the office, you'll need to pick a theme with enough options so that you won't run out of names. If you pick planets, for example, you won't be able to have more than ten desktops without using planet names you heard on Star Trek reruns.

Some good themes we've seen include:

- Car parts
- Planets
- Greek alphabet
- Rock bands
- Flowers
- Geographic locations (states, mountains, lakes)

- Colors (again, not too many options here unless you run a paint department)
- Elements

Fourth, consider a generation-based naming scheme. For example, when a client does a technology refresh, give a standard name with a two-digit number. For example, Alpha, Beta, Gamma generations will have Alpha01, Alpha02, Beta01, etc. So you know that Beta machines are all newer than all Alpha machines. This might not be worth the trouble.

Fifth, you might use a department name along with a counter. Sales01, sales 02, finance01, finance02, etc. This works best in large offices. As with personal names, you don't want to find yourself with machine finance02 in the sales department.

Plan on Retiring Machines

One of the key things to remember with computers is that machines die, get old, become obsolete, and are retired. So the names need to allow for this. Ideally, you will be able to retire a name and not reuse it. Or at least not reuse it for a few years. This works well with Station01 ... Station99. It's not as successful with the Seven Dwarfs.

Server01 might be a SQL server this year and an Exchange server next year. But after that, it might be a donation to the local charity. So the name Server01 should be retired and another server added to the end of the machine list.

This policy – not reusing machine names – saves confusion in the long run. This is particularly true with RMM tools and PSA systems.

Copyright © 2014 Karl W. Palachuk

You don't want to have sales03 in your paper documentation be different from sales03 in your PSA and even different from sales03 in your RMM tool.

So think of machine names as single-use resources.

We have a spec sheet for machine names. That's where we lay out the plan for machine names. In some cases (e.g., flowers or Greek alphabet), we find a good list on the Internet and put a copy in the network documentation binder (See Volume Four in this series.) That way a tech on site can just look up a new name and not waste any time.

It is important to keep track of all machines on a network. We have layers and layers of documentation on this. As I just mentioned, there's paper documentation, PSA documentation, and RMM documentation. Keeping this straight is a lot easier if you never reuse a machine name.

And therefore, it makes a lot of sense to plan out your machine names as early as possible. And when you get new clients, set up a policy and begin putting new machines into the new naming scheme as you can.

Implementation Notes

The most basic element of implementation is to simply write 1-2 sentences explaining the naming scheme for each client. This should live in their network documentation binder. You might also put a note in the PSA.

Machine Spec Sheets will of course help in this process.

3 and 3

Three Take-Aways from This Chapter:

1. Think of machine names as single-use resources.

2. Get in the habit of using machines names that are as compatible as needed for all the systems you touch. e.g., 15 characters or less.

3. Involve the client if they're interested – but guide their choices.

Three Action Steps for Your Company:

1. _____

   _____

2. _____

   _____

3. _____

   _____

Copyright © 2014 Karl W. Palachuk

Copyright © 2014 Karl W. Palachuk

3

Schedules and Timelines for Running Your Company

True success comes from working on priorities and letting priorities govern your day instead of a calendar. Fine. But the reality is that you also need to live by a few schedules. And, more importantly, most employees will rely on the calendar more than priorities.

(On the topic of priorities vs. calendars, see *The Power of Focus* by Jack Canfield and First Things First by Stephen R. Covey, A. Roger Merrill, and Rebecca R. Merrill.)

When you do need to use a calendar, it is best to lay things out well in advance. If you just put them in outlook, you'll get a reminder 1-3 days in advance (or 15 minutes). That generally doesn't work. For big things, you need to set the schedule, plan on it, and make it happen.

Calendars fail for the most part because people don't actually refer back to them. Items are set, but not set in stone. So they get moved around and forgotten. This gets to the basics of management. If it's important, do it. If it's not important, don't schedule it.

When your staff see that you don't make something a priority, they won't make it a priority.

So what kinds of things are we talking about? I won't try to give an exhaustive list of the things you might schedule, but I'll give you some

Copyright © 2014 Karl W. Palachuk

examples. How you handle the scheduling of various task depends on the task, and who is responsible for the scheduling.

In Volume One we talked about celebrating birthdays and anniversaries. That schedule is probably kept in Outlook, but could also be listed on your managed service grid for tracking your clients (an Excel spreadsheet, also discussed in Volume One of this series). That tracking is done by the office manager.

Note the important elements for tracking this:

1) Who is responsible?

2) Where is the definitive schedule information stored (e.g., in an Excel document on \\companyshare\operations\procedures...)

3) Where else is this information stored for ease of use (e.g., printout on bulletin board)

4) What is the process/procedure for updating this information?

I'm going to give some example schedules and processes. After you see a few of these, the "process" of managing a scheduling process should be very easy to replicate.

Example One: Quarterly or Annual Reviews

Background: I'm a big believer in quarterly or annual reviews for employees. Yes, you see them every day. But it is always nice to get a formal review about what's working and what's not. This is a perfect example of something that is easy to put off - with bad consequences. If you announce reviews and then put them off and put them off, then employees conclude that it's really not important to you.

Copyright © 2014 Karl W. Palachuk

Process: The office manager creates a personnel spreadsheet that includes the employee's name, date of hire, last review date, and next scheduled review. (Note: The actual review process is the subject of a chapter in Volume Two of this series.)

The office manager first determines which dates and times the manager would like to set aside for reviews. This often works best if you pick a standard time slot and let the office manager fill as needed. For example, you might do employee reviews on Tuesday mornings. The office manager will need access to the manager's calendar. Once times are established, the office manager contacts technicians and other staff to schedule reviews.

Reviews should be scheduled far enough in advance for the manager to review the employee's file, write up a paragraph or two, fill out the company's standard review form, and generally be prepared for the review itself.

When the review is completed, any action steps that are required should flow to tasks in Outlook or the company's PSA system. For example, the employee might be getting a raise or increased hours. The employee might be eligible for company-paid training. You need a process to make sure that decisions made as a result of employee reviews turn into actions within the company.

Note: I have come to believe that reviews should be separated from raises, but many companies still handle them together. You should have more reviews than raises. ☺

The office manager is informed that the review has taken place, updates the Excel spreadsheet, and creates a tickler to schedule again in three months or twelve months. You can see that a nice flow chart for this process makes it very smooth.

Copyright © 2014 Karl W. Palachuk

Example Two: Monday Morning Meetings

Background: When your company gets to a certain size, you might find that you are all running around and don't see each other much anymore. You need to maintain/build a company culture. Part of how you do that is to get together in a "huddle" at least once a week. It doesn't have to be long. But you should create a forum to chat with one another, get to know each other as people, and keep the work focused on what needs to be done to stay profitable.

Process: For example, you might have a meeting of the managers each week, followed by a meeting of the company as a whole, and then perhaps the individual departments. Again, these don't have to take long. If the managers work closely together all the time, maybe they don't need a meeting every week.

Let's say you have a schedule like this:

- Managers meeting = 8:00 AM

- Company Meeting = 8:30 AM

- Tech Team Meeting = 9:00 AM

The key thing here is consistency. If you schedule a meeting every week, **hold the meeting**. If you cancel it every other week, then don't schedule it. Perhaps impromptu meetings work.

You'll notice that, even with a very small staff, there are people who will "save up" issues to bring up at the company meeting. If you schedule and cancel, you frustrate these people because they thought they had an outlet for their concern, but now it's shelved for another week.

You can say, "Well, it shouldn't be that way. Just speak up." But you have to remember that we all have different and unique personalities. Part of building a team is recognizing these differences and helping

Copyright © 2014 Karl W. Palachuk

people learn to work together. That includes YOU being aware of the kinds of people on your team.

Example Three: Monthly Maintenance

Background: You should run a "Monthly Maintenance" procedure on every contract client every month. If you have a Remote Monitoring and Management (RMM) system, then your list of chores is very short. That's because many things are monitored 24x7 in real time, such as disc space. But you will still need to go to the client's office, shake their hand, look at their server, test the backup, and do some kind of checkup. This is partly tune-up and partly client relations.

Process: For starters, you need a monthly maintenance checklist. That's a list of things you will monitor or do every single month as part of the preventive maintenance that makes managed services work. If you need a place to start, check out my Newly Revised 68-Point Checklist. It is included with the download materials for this book.

Once you have your standard checklist, you will refine it for each client. Clients have different backups, different databases, different network setups. So their checklists need to be customized.

You will need to execute four things every month with regard to monthly maintenances: 1) Execute the monthly maintenance checklist at each client; 2) Revise all monthly maintenance checklists as needed; 3) Make sure the revised MMC is published appropriately and "ready to go" for the next month; and 4) Each MMC must be filed away for future reference.

Obviously, you have a serious time crunch here. No matter whether you have ten clients or a hundred, you need to execute the MMC every month. Someone needs to maintain a calendar so that MMC

Copyright © 2014 Karl W. Palachuk

visits are spaced properly. Clients look puzzled if you show up on the 27th of February and then again on March 1st. This scheduling might be done by the office manager, but is more likely to be done by the tech department.

It's a good idea to keep a calendar of when MMCs were executed at each client so you can look back very easily. You almost never need this information, but it's handy when you do.

The revision process is very simple, but needs to be done! If you skip it, you just create more work down the road. Revisions include things like noting that the c:\ drive is too full for logs, so the logs have been moved to the d:\ drive. If that happens, the checklist needs to point to the right place. Normally, revisions are little things like that. Occasionally they are major, such as a new backup procedure.

In a perfect world, the checklist will be updated as the last item on the checklist. But if the tech is onsite, then it will likely wait until he gets back to the office. The problem there is that checklists tend to get thrown on a pile because something more important comes up. If that happens, you need to set aside a date or deadline to get them updated.

As for "publishing," I simply mean that the revised document should be posted on your internal SharePoint site or uploaded to the PSA. We publish these in .pdf format so that they can be accessed and printed off from any computer, including a client server with no Word program installed.

Finally, you need to file away your MMCs. You might file them all together for one month, or put each one into the appropriate client folder. Which you choose depends on which you think will be more useful down the road. You will need to refer to these when you are looking for problems across clients and when investigating something with a specific client. For technicians, having them all in one place is probably easiest. For billing and client relations, having each client's checklists in the client folder works best. You decide.

All MMCs should be executed by a certain date. They should be updated and published by a certain date. And they should be filed away by a certain date. Every month. No exceptions. Determine who will be responsible for each of these schedules and develop a process.

Example Four: Patch Management

Background: Whether you have a professional RMM tool or you roll your own with Windows Updates, you need to have a process for applying patches. It can be pretty well automated, but you should still check up on it on a regular basis. And just in case I need to say this: You should **absolutely** be applying patches, fixes, and updates to you clients' machines!

We all know that Microsoft security patches come out once a month unless something really nasty is happening. You can stay tuned into these updates at

http://technet.microsoft.com/en-au/security/bulletin/

So you need a schedule for applying (or not applying) these patches. Some MSPs take the view that only specific, relevant patches should be applied. We take the opposite view. We think you should apply everything unless you have a specific reason NOT to. The days when patches blew up the world and destroyed things are pretty much in the past. Still, some caution is useful.

As a general rule, we apply all patches. But we don't do so immediately. Sometimes patches are recalled, or black-listed by our RMM tool. In such cases, we are glad that we proceed slowly.

Copyright © 2014 Karl W. Palachuk

We recommend that you schedule patches to be applied Sunday night. If there's a backup, schedule after the backups are complete. If you apply all patches every Sunday night, then all machines should be up to spec when you come to work on Monday. In the rare instance when a machine hangs or is waiting for an "enter" key, you can take care of it first thing.

In the old days, before RMM and before Microsoft patches were as reliable as they have become, we had a three-tiered process:

1) Wait a day to see if the patch is recalled

2) On the next available weekend, deploy the patch to our servers/workstations

3) On the next weekend, (assuming no problems) deploy to client servers/workstations

As with many processes, it doesn't matter exactly what your procedure is, **as long as you have a procedure in place**.

For the most part, the patch management "schedule" runs automatically, especially if you have an RMM tool. Still, someone should be responsible to make sure that things are flowing the way you want and that you're not missing any big patches.

Those are somewhat long examples, but the point is to show you that you can have a systematic approach to success. If you put these processes in place when you're small, then you'll have to fine-tune as you grow. There are plenty of other schedules and calendars in any business (holidays, tax deadlines, government paperwork, insurance, etc.). Some simply show up in the mail. Others need to be managed.

Once you create a system for one scheduling process, the second is easy, the third is easier, and so forth.

Copyright © 2014 Karl W. Palachuk

And you never have to be surprised when something shows up on your calendar!

Copyright © 2014 Karl W. Palachuk

3 and 3

Three Take-Aways from This Chapter:

1. Document the "big" events in your business that need to be scheduled.

2. Determine who will be responsible for each of these major events..

3. Determine how you will measure the success of scheduling company-wide activities.

Three Action Steps for Your Company:

1. _____

   _____

2. _____

   _____

3. _____

   _____

Copyright © 2014 Karl W. Palachuk

4

Working in Real Time

One of the hardest things for people to do is to keep good track of their time. At the same time, this is one of the key elements of success, both in tech support delivery and business generally.

Time tracking is absolutely critical to profitability. Unfortunately, it's one of those things that everyone knows they should do, but don't always get around to.

There are several pieces to working in real time.

First, the definition: **Working in real time means that you enter your labor into your PSA system as soon as you complete a job.** In fact, it is preferred that you log on and enter time as the last step in each job. That way, even if it only takes a few minutes, the time to enter time is part of the job!

This is completely legitimate. If the job is billable, then the time to enter time is billable. If the job is covered under managed service, then the time appears in the system for that specific client/ticket. In either case, it is critical that the time is properly associated with the ticket so that you can run reports and determine the profitability of each job and client.

We use a hosted PSA system so we can log on from any computer at any client's office and enter time. Before we had a PSA system, I used a simple web-based form that emailed job notes to me. This included

Copyright © 2014 Karl W. Palachuk

start/stop times, a description of the work accomplished, and notes about any hardware or software that were delivered.

I made a habit of filling out this simple form after each job, and required my techs to do the same thing. Before that, I required that they sit down and fill out a printed form before leaving the client. Same information, just a different delivery method.

The alternative to working in real time is that you have to have **perfect recall** or **perfect notes**. Perfect recall is perfectly impossible. Whether it's you or your employees, mistakes will be made. Recall will be wrong. Whole hours will disappear. Job notes will be lost.

Perfect notes are much better. BUT if you take perfect notes, why not take an extra 3-5 minutes and enter them into the system? The alternative is to wait until after work and then sit down and enter all your time at once. This will then take an hour that can't be billed or properly allocated to jobs!

Implementation Notes

The easiest way to implement the policy of working in real time is to base employee pay on the reports you get from your PSA system. This means you need a ticket for "admin" time so that you can track employee time between 8 AM and 5 PM with no gaps or overlaps.

This is also a GREAT way to find out if you have techs putting 4-6 hours a day on internal admin tasks versus client-facing tickets.

As with everything else, you'll need to make the decision, announce it, implement it, and then build an atmosphere in which everyone supports everyone else to be successful.

Copyright © 2014 Karl W. Palachuk

Benefits

Here are the key benefits of working in real time:

1) You have a better sense of where you are with each client/ticket

2) Important notes are not forgotten

3) Time is entered accurately

4) Employee hours are accurate

5) Everyone on the team can see the accurate status of a job

6) With accurate time entry, you can get accurate calculations of **billability**, profit per hour billed, cost to support a client, backlog, etc. None of these key metrics is possible if you are just guessing at the hours worked and how they're allocated.

Forms

If you are using a manual process, you need a simple form. In the modern world, this really should be a mobile app or a web page. In either case, the form elements are:

- Client

- Ticket / Job Title

- Desktop / User

- Technician

- Date

- Start Time

Copyright © 2014 Karl W. Palachuk

- Stop Time

- Adjustment for time if necessary

- Work was on site / remote

- Notes on work performed. This should include key information about what happened, notes from third party support, and all information needed to discuss this matter with the client or others as needed. It should also include notes on the delivery of products and any client requests for quotes or other information for the sales department.

- Internal notes regarding billing (not for clients)

Of course a PSA system will automate all of this. Most PSAs have some mobile app or mobile interface.

One of the coolest things about working in real time is that you get a steady stream of emails all day showing how your business is progressing and your people are taking care of your clients. Ping-ping-ping.

Copyright © 2014 Karl W. Palachuk

3 and 3

Three Take-Aways from This Chapter:

1. To make sure your records are accurate you either need to work in real time, keep perfect notes, or use perfect recall.

2. The most important reports you can get from your PSA rely on having your staff enter their time in real time.

3. All excuses for not working in real time amount to this: People are not in the habit. Once they *are* in the habit, it is automatic and easy.

Three Action Steps for Your Company:

1. _____

   _____

2. _____

   _____

3. _____

   _____

Copyright © 2014 Karl W. Palachuk

Copyright © 2014 Karl W. Palachuk

5

Used Equipment and Warranties

Some lessons we learn again and again - until we're tired of being bit in the butt!

Over time, most technicians come around to accepting that you should only sell new equipment and you should encourage every client to keep a warranty on all hardware (and a Maintenance agreement on all software).

These seem like different topics, but they're very much related to one another, and to your profit.

Overview

As techno-goobers, we tend to have boxes filled with old network cards, modems, video cards, memory, hard drives, and all the juicy goodness that makes computers fun. We sometimes grab one of these devices and throw it into a computer. For fun. For troubleshooting. Cuz we're nerds.

And that's fine for US, in our shop, with our computers. But client systems are another story altogether.

There are extreme rare exceptions, but as a general rule **You should never install used equipment in any client system.**

If you waste four hours of your time finding drivers for an NE2000 compatible NIC on your Windows 7 box, that's just good fun. If you

Copyright © 2014 Karl W. Palachuk

blow out the hard drive or have to set the O.S. back to a previous restore point, that's part of game. (For the younger folks, the NE2000 compatible network card was an industry standard like the Hayes compatible modem and the Epson 9-pin printer. The point is: It's old.)

But if you do these things at a client's office, 1) You look like an idiot, and 2) You're losing money. I've said it before, but let me be very clear: You have to decide whether this is your hobby or a business. If it's a business, you can easily put yourself in the position of never selling used equipment. Just don't do it.

Every once in a while we come across an old video card (or NIC or sound card or whatever) that just won't work. Can't find the reason. Can't find the drivers. Whatever the case may be: It won't work. **Throw It Away!**

The thing about used equipment is that most of it works most of the time. But the probability that it won't work goes up when a client is involved. Murphy goes along on that job every time. Just don't do it.

As with many decisions, you need to break it down to dollars and hours. A new video card is $50 plus your one hour minimum to install. Some old piece of junk might be $25 or "free" and take two hours labor to get right. Unless something goes wrong. Then it might be another two hours.

How much time will you spend to save $25? Your answer had **better be** less than 15 minutes. If you only charge $100/hour, then $25 = 15 minutes. Spending an extra hour to make old junk work is hardly ever worth it.

And if you're successful, you have an old piece of equipment without a warranty that cost almost as much as the new one.

Copyright © 2014 Karl W. Palachuk

Remember that you need to guard your time like the precious commodity it is. If you are completely successful with used equipment 90% of the time and only have problems ten percent of the time, you still have lost money. You are spinning your wheels on unproductive labor rather than engaged in delightful, interesting, billable work.

Warranties are a related topic. Let's just talk about hardware here and not maintenance agreements for business applications.

The key thing about a warranty is that you severely limit your exposure. When a problem arises, you call the manufacturer, they send a replacement, and you install it. Or, better yet, they install it. You manage that relationship. But they do as much work as possible.

Between diagnosis, dealing with warranty support, and installing new components, you can probably limit your time on a warranty replacement to one hour total in most cases.

New equipment, especially new equipment that ships with a three year warranty, is FAR less likely to have any problems. We actually cover the labor on equipment that's under warranty if the client bought it from us. The reason is simple: We almost never have to spend labor on new equipment under warranty, and it gives the client a strong sense that we're just taking care of stuff. Clients like NOT getting additional bills.

We can only do this with new, warrantied equipment.

Implementation Notes

There are two pieces to this puzzle. One is an internal policy and one is in your service agreement.

The Internal Policy is simple:

> "It is the policy of this company that we do not sell used equipment. This includes refurbished equipment. If a new component is delivered to a client and installed in a machine, that component belongs to the client and may not be removed and returned to stock for resale. It is used. We will only quote new hardware with a minimum of one year warranty."

The second piece goes in your managed service agreement. (If you need sample agreements, see the book *Service Agreements for SMB Consultants*.) Here's a place to start:

> "Warranties. All equipment (network equipment, servers, printers, desktop computers, laptop computer, etc.) must be under an original manufacturer's warranty, or some other similar warranty or extended service plan in order to be covered by this Agreement. Work performed on equipment that is not under warranty will not be covered under this Agreement. All such work will be billed according to the rates and terms of the Agreement."

. . .

> "Hardware Support: In addition to the maintenance of the operating system and software, above, Consultant agrees to provide hardware support for all equipment that is purchased from Consultant and covered under this Agreement, provided that such equipment is less than three years old and is under manufacturer's warranty."

Note: I'm not an attorney. Have your service agreement reviewed by an attorney. I'm not responsible for anything you do. Blah, blah, blah.

Benefits

The primary benefit of this policy is that you will do a lot less work on hardware related items. To me that's a real benefit. Hardware work today is the least interesting part about this business.

Another benefit is that you'll make more money! Okay, that might be the primary benefit.

You'll make money from warranties for three reasons. First, you'll sell good equipment that doesn't break. So you'll spend less labor fixing things after you've been paid. Second, you can make money on extended warranties. If clients want to keep old machines, they need to either pay for hardware fixes or pay for an extended warranty. Third, you will make money from work that's not covered by warranty.

Eventually, when machines become expensive to maintain (see the next chapter), clients will decide to upgrade.

Overall, these policies will make computer maintenance a lot easier and more trouble-free. Clients should not be under the impression that computers and always a hassle and break down all the time. You can show them a brighter, more beautiful future!

Forms

See the sample policy statement above and the sample warranty language for your service agreements, above.

Copyright © 2014 Karl W. Palachuk

It is also helpful to keep track of the warranty status of machines in the Network Documentation Binder (see Volume Four in this series) or in your PSA.

When you have a service ticket that is for un-warrantied hardware, be sure to change it to be billable labor.

Copyright © 2014 Karl W. Palachuk

3 and 3

Three Take-Aways from This Chapter:

1. Just don't sell used (or refurbished) equipment. Just don't.

2. Reduce client costs by covering hardware-related labor when the hardware was purchased from you and is under warranty.

3. Take note of how few things fail as you work with newer and newer equipment under warranty.

Three Action Steps for Your Company:

1. _____

   _____

2. _____

   _____

3. _____

   _____

Copyright © 2014 Karl W. Palachuk

6

Hardware Replacement and Upgrade Policy

When do you replace hardware? Well, that's more complicated than it appears at first. There's the "ideal" policy, the reality of dealing with clients. And then we have the reality of dealing with clients in the worst recession in sixty years.

General Rule for Success: "We Like To See . . ."

Let me just take a sidebar here and explain a powerful rule of success if you are a computer consultant (or any kind of consultant). You need to have a *philosophy* about how things are done. In some way, this is a core belief that leads us to create all these other policies.

It boils down to this: The combined total of all the advice you give will move your clients in the right direction. It will give them better performance from their computers, more efficiency from their employees, and save them money in the long run.

Every month we celebrate client anniversaries. We have clients who have been with us five years, ten years, fifteen years, and more. When I look back on all the advice that's been given and taken, I can honestly say that we saved them money "in the long run" because of our advice.

Newbies to our company don't understand how we can have so few service requests. We have weeks where basically nothing happens.

Copyright © 2014 Karl W. Palachuk

That's because we are very firm in pushing our philosophy about hardware, software, licensing, maintenance, and spending money wisely (which might mean spending more in the short term).

The key phrase to memorize here is **We like to see . . .** because it gives clients confidence that you have a big-picture philosophy about how things are done. We like to see hardware replaced every three years. We like to see Exchange on a hosted platform. We like to see point-in-time backups. We like to see a documentation folder for each machine.

When you go into a client with strong philosophies about how things are done, they feel more comfortable relying on you to give them good advice!

As for Hardware Replacement and Upgrades . . .

There are two major policies here. First, there's a policy regarding upgrades. That is, upgrading existing hardware. Second, there's the philosophy regarding replacement of hardware.

Upgrading Existing Hardware

This used to be more of an issue in the "old days" when 1) Technology kept improving at a fast pace, 2) Things broke, and 3) Components were installed separately.

Today, most of the core components are built into the motherboard. LAN card, Video, sound, printer, RS-232, USB: It's all onboard. So if something goes wrong you normally just call the manufacturer because it's covered by the warranty. (See the last chapter.)

But, aside from that, *things don't break*. Well, rarely. I don't remember the last time an onboard LAN went bad, or a sound card

Copyright © 2014 Karl W. Palachuk

or video. I think I recall one bad LAN port in the last ten years. And all I really recall is that someone had taped over it with a label that said to use the add-on LAN card. So maybe it wasn't bad at all.

We used to get faster and faster modems. But now 56K is the top. You either get one or you don't. LAN ports have been 100 MB or 1 GB for so long that no one ever upgrades. Sound is onboard. Very few people want an upgrade in the business environment, unless they're doing something special. Every machine has five or more USB ports.

The point is: We almost never have to address upgrading existing hardware. But when we do, here's our policy:

General

It is this company's core belief that a business class machine's useful life is 3 years.

Upgrading Hardware

We do not upgrade hardware in machines that are more than 3 years old. If we're looking for a manufacturer part, we end up spending a lot of time trying to find the right thing and get it ordered. We almost always lost money once we consider the labor involved in getting such parts.

In addition, we are much more likely to experience additional problems once we start replacing stuff. For example, we've had a motherboard go bad after upgrading memory. Yes, we've done it a million times. But suddenly something goes bad and it's an issue that has to be addressed.

The only two possible exceptions are:

Copyright © 2014 Karl W. Palachuk

1) A retrofit (not upgrade) of a business critical machine in an attempt to keep it alive long enough for its replacement to come on line.

2) We have explained our policy to a client and they are willing to pay for both our time to find the correct parts and all time for all installation and troubleshooting of issues arising from that installation.

So far, we haven't had too many clients that are so endeared to a machine that they select option 2.

Replacement Hardware

Note, please, that this discussion involves all hardware except printers. That means that we're talking about servers, desktops, laptops, routers, firewalls, switches, . . . everything.

Printers are an exception because we tend to sell business class HP printers, and they never die. One time we had a client who built their annual conference registration system around HP Laserjet 4 printers (a wise choice). I had bought a used HP4 from a client. So it was 5+ years old when I bought it. When I decided to move to a faster printer, I sold it to this client for their conference registration system. Five years later, they retired that system and there was my old printer in the pile, in perfect working order. Finally donated to charity along with the rest.

As for everything else . . . Our general rule is that a business class machine's useful life is 3 years. There are several reasons for this.

First, we sell business class machines. So they're built to last that long. They're built with better parts and better processes. They're inspected more carefully. And they really should last three years trouble-free.

Copyright © 2014 Karl W. Palachuk

This is true of HP. It's true of Lenovo. It's even true of Dell – if you buy business class machines.

You can take a "home" grade PC (or low-grade server) and boost the memory, boost the cache, boost the hard drive, etc. You can spend just as much as a business class machine, but you'll have an upgraded home machine. It won't be designed to last three years. You need to start with good equipment and figure out how to reach your price point. Never start with cheap equipment and spend your way up, because it will never become business class.

Second, we sell only servers and workstations that come with a 3-year warranty. For everything else (firewalls, switches, etc.) we require at least a one-year warranty and we really push the three years. We always quote equipment with three years' worth of warranty, whether it's standard or an upgrade.

Our managed service agreements require that all covered equipment has to be under warranty. If not, all labor is billable. There are two very simple reasons for this:

1) Equipment designed to have a three year warranty almost never has any issues within the first three years. In fact, it also never has issues within the first five years! It's "business class" and just works.

2) In the fourth or fifth year, under extended warranty, we can still just call the manufacturer and say, "Come fix your stuff."

Third, technology marches on! Whether a client wants to admit it or not, you have to upgrade sometime. Old machines get slow. They get bogged down with lots of programs. They get asked to do more than they were intended to do. Hard drives begin to slow down because of re-reads and re-writes. Older machines have fan issues, even if they're not obvious, so they're hotter and slower.

Copyright © 2014 Karl W. Palachuk

AND all the equipment in your office has to work together. When you replace a desktop here and a desktop there, pretty soon the server is the slowest machine in the office. It's working overtime just to keep up with all those fast desktops.

Network equipment also gets old. Ports go bad. But more importantly, older chipsets are slower than newer chipsets. New kinds of protocols come into existence and the routers and switches don't know what to do with them. VOIP is a GREAT example of this. Very often, manufacturers will put a 100 MB port on a firewall that can't possible pump out data faster then 30 or 40 MB. Yeah, you get a link light. But you don't get the data flow you're paying for.

That approach worked great when you were moving from a 1.5MB T1 to a 6 MB DSL line. But with a 70 GB cable connection or 100 GB Fiber, you are totally wasting your bandwidth potential and slowing down everything in the office.

Older, slower equipment is just going to get older and slower. Period.

A philosophy of regular three-year upgrades will always keep your client working efficiently with quality equipment.

There's a very weird mentality with equipment. Sometimes we find ourselves saying, "It still works." Well, yeah. So what? The first Compaq Proliant I ever installed with Windows NT 3.5 is still working today. Pentium, baby! With a blazing 96 MB of RAM. 16 GB SCSI drives. It takes ten minutes just to POST. But it works!

The fact that you can turn on a stereo amplifier built in 1974 and it works is NOT impressive. It's solid state. It should just work. But does it give you the performance you want?

A switch (or even a hub) that's five, ten, or fifteen years old will "work." It will turn on. The lights will blink. Data will flow. But that

Copyright © 2014 Karl W. Palachuk

doesn't mean it's a good idea to use that equipment in the backbone of a client's network.

A five year old server will turn on. It will load the O.S. Lights will blink. Data will flow. But that doesn't mean it's a good idea to use that equipment in the backbone of a client's network.

The Sales Pitch

Many clients accept the three year rule. This is due, in large part, to the fact that we harp on it all the time. We remind them of the age of their machines. Sometimes we even label machines with the year they were new. We quote replacements for three year old equipment. We encourage the clients to officially adopt a three year replacement policy. And when machines are absolutely brand new, we remind them that it will be old in three years.

I would say that "most" clients accept this policy. Most of them allow us to replace servers in three years. So, while they might extend the warranty for a year, they begin getting quotes to replace it at the same time. Most clients try to adopt similar policies with desktops, but they tend to be closer to the four year mark.

And a four year old desktop is not horrible these days.

But, as you know, the new desktop machine that replaced it is blazingly faster! I love projects that require a decision maker to sit down at three or more of their employee machines and work on a project. They see how painfully slow they are making their employees work. It really helps them see that we're not just pushing hardware to make money.

It's funny how little attention is given to desktop machines, given that they are the most important productivity tool for 90% of all employees in our clients' offices.

Copyright © 2014 Karl W. Palachuk

So we're not just pushing hardware sales. We really are working to make them more efficient and profitable. This policy is not meant to serve us. It is meant to serve the client. After all, when we're working on an old, slow piece of crap, we're getting paid by the hour. With that policy in place, we'd make a lot more money working on old equipment!

I know you know how it is. We are so "into" technology that we can't stand being on old, slow machines. But some people somehow convince themselves that they're saving money.

You need to believe this philosophy deep in your heart: Old machines cost money! You need to speak this philosophy when talking to employees and clients. You need to work it into your web site, your newsletters, and all of your client conversations.

"We like to see these machines replaced every three years."

Copyright © 2014 Karl W. Palachuk

3 and 3

Three Take-Aways from This Chapter:

1. Your mantra is: We sell business class equipment, and we expect it to perform perfectly for three years. Repeat to clients and employees.

2. Build processes and messaging around the three-year target.

3. Just because old equipment "works" doesn't mean you want to build your business on it.

Three Action Steps for Your Company:

1. _____

_____

2. _____

_____

3. _____

_____

Copyright © 2014 Karl W. Palachuk

Copyright © 2014 Karl W. Palachuk

7

Software Upgrade Policy

In Chapter Twenty-Six we'll look at Activating and Registering Client Software and Hardware. And in the last chapter we talked about your Hardware Replacement and Upgrade Policy. This is a very different Software topic.

You need a policy (or at least a philosophy) about **software upgrades**, even if you don't sell software. Because it is central to the success of our clients, we need to give them good guidance. Here I'm going to address three topics regarding software upgrades: Philosophy, What you sell, and patching.

Software Upgrade Philosophy

Perhaps the most important message you can send your clients about software is a consistent approach to upgrades. When something's new, the only decision is whether to buy it. But when it gets older you have to decide what to do about "generations" of software. I'll use the Microsoft office suite as my primary example since it is in most client offices.

Clients inherently know that life is easier if everyone has the same version of Office. This is particularly true of older software. Office XP and Office 2010 are not compatible. You can open Office XP docs in

Copyright © 2014 Karl W. Palachuk

2010, but you have to "save as" the old format in order to open with XP again. Once someone updates the file, it's all over.

Macros are particularly troublesome since Visual Basic also changes with each software generation.

Even things that are supposed to be 100% compatible are not. In our book business, we have seen that complicated documents we save in Word 2010 have problems opening successfully in Word 2007, even though they are supposed to be the same format.

Realistically, many offices cannot afford to upgrade everyone's Office Suite just because one person got the new version. Having more than one version can cause a serious reduction in productivity for some offices. Each has to decide what it's worth. As a result **we're okay with skipping a generation**. This makes the upgrade process more affordable. And, if the client buys open licenses, they can legally install the current version or the most immediate previous version. So staying in sync is easy and doesn't cost more.

Ideally, we like clients to agree to **only skip one generation**. Look at your own clients. The handful with "that one" Access 97 database have a hundred times more trouble with Microsoft Office issues than any of your other clients. They don't see the difference because they only see their office, but you see the difference all the time.

When companies commit to only skipping one generation, it means they have to shell out some money up front for new software every five years or so. But in the long run, they definitely save money. So

you have to work to convince them to keep up with the upgrade policy. And, whenever a new version of Office is released, you have to remind them of the "best practice" in this area.

Another important policy is to **match up the hardware generation with the operating system generation**. For example, we will not install Server 2003 on new hardware. Period. It doesn't have the right drivers. It might not recognize some of the new components. It certainly can't take advantage of the newer features (in this example, 64 bit processing).

By the same token, we won't put Server 2012 on a five year old machine. We don't want to install a 2012 operating system on any machine older than 2011. The hardware won't be beefy enough. It won't have all the components to take advantage of new features (like hardware-level virtualization). And it often can't be upgraded to provide reasonable performance without a huge cost. See the last chapter.

Summary: Pay attention to the software "generation" and develop your philosophy about upgrades. You need to balance client needs with costs. For us that means it's okay to skip a generation, but don't skip two generations. And we like to see the hardware and operating system from the same generation.

What You Sell

We have three primary policies about what we sell regarding software.

First, we sell the latest operating system.

Second, we decide between OEM and Open Licensing depending on the client's needs.

Copyright © 2014 Karl W. Palachuk

Third, we sell other upgrades when they're really needed.

Many years ago I was asked to give a second opinion to a prospect. They had purchased several new computers, which shipped with the new Windows 98 operating system. Their "consultant" had quoted additional software costs and labor to remove the Windows 98 and install Windows 95. His reasoning: Windows 95 is stable and no one ever trusts the first generation of a Microsoft product.

The client asked me what I recommend. Of course I said that I would never replace a brand new O.S. with something that's three years old and based on old technology. This amounted to a consultant who only knew one O.S. and was afraid to support the new one. That's just an unsustainable business model.

We sell the latest operating system. I'll be honest – Windows 8 is my least favorite Windows O.S. ever. But I use it and I sell it. Even in the days of Vista, we sold Vista. Techno-goobers and pundits didn't like it, and it was a P.R. nightmare for Microsoft. But as an operating system, it worked great. The primary reason we never had issues with Vista: We only sold it on new hardware designed for Vista.

When you don't sell the latest operating system, you deprive your clients of many new features, and you increase their overall support costs.

We don't upgrade just to upgrade, but when we sell a new computer, we always choose the latest operating system. Through the whole fiasco of trying to make Windows XP live forever, we simply sold the latest, greatest, and most secure operating system available. That policy never steered us wrong.

As for **OEM vs. Licensing**, we have changed our tune. We used to drink lots of Microsoft Kool-Aid and push licensing. And for many clients it made a lot of sense. But for smaller clients, Open Licensing has fewer advantages.

Here's the argument for Open Licensing from Microsoft:

1) You get the latest office suite (or operating system). If you want to use the previous version, you could install instead.

2) You have a perpetual license so you never have to un-install the software.

3) If you buy two years of software assurance, you can get the next version at no additional charge (*if* it's released during that 2-year period).

4) Legally, you can uninstall the software from one system and install on another. So, if your hard drive or mother board fails, you can legally install this software on another machine. You can't do that with OEM. It dies when the machine dies.

Open License makes great sense for larger organizations. You can deploy it en masse and know that everyone is legal. You can maintain consistency throughout the organization, which saves more money over the long run in large companies. Re-installing as needed is simple and you don't have to worry about whether its legal. Overall, management and maintenance is easier with Open Licensing.

With OEM, the key drawback is that you're buying something that will die. Not might, will die. It lives with the machine. So despite client claims that they can do whatever they want, they can't. Luckily, Microsoft licensing authentication has gotten very good, so you spend less time convincing clients that you can't break the license agreement for them.

Copyright © 2014 Karl W. Palachuk

The key advantage to OEM is that it's a lot cheaper. A secondary advantage is that you can sell one license at a time. Open License has a five-license minimum.

With regard to price: When you sell OEM, you have to tell the client that it's a bit of a gamble. As long as the machine lasts, they can use that license. If the machine lives ten years, they can use that license for ten years. Since you only sell business class machines with a three year warranty, they are guaranteed at least three years of life. But if the machine dies in the fourth year, they have to buy Office again. For most clients this is a complete non-issue. Even if they keep the machine for five years, the chances that they will have a failure that requires the purchase of another copy of Office is pretty slim.

With regard to the five-license minimum: For really small companies that buy 1-4 computers a year, they will have a tough time staying eligible for the Open Licensing unless the office licenses are bought at the same time as the Server licenses, and they have software assurance so that they can add additional licenses for two years. This becomes a simple math problem. And a pain in the neck when that Software Assurance expires.

The bottom line is that OEM is usually the best choice for very small clients and Open Licensing is better for larger clients. The big exception would be small clients who are Not-for-Profit organizations. They can use Tech Soup to get software at **extremely** low prices, so they can afford to buy 10 or 15 copies and be legal everywhere. (See http://www.techsoup.org.)

Patches, Fixes, and Updates

Finally, we get to patches, fixes, and updates. This one is pretty easy: Install 'em! Unless there's a major reason not to, we install all the

Copyright © 2014 Karl W. Palachuk

latest patches, fixes, and updates. This is true for operating systems and software.

Just do it.

Most updates are minor and only affect microscopic pieces of the overall code. These are delivered via Automatic Updates or by manually running Windows Updates. We use our RMM, of course, to push the most important updates. They currently deploy security updates, but will be expanding to additional updates as well.

I know some people freak out about every update that comes along. But realistically, 99.999% of the time, nothing bad ever happens. So we don't have a policy based on the exception to the rule. We have a policy based on the rule: Apply the latest updates.

The reason is extremely simple. Call tech support (for Windows, Office, QuickBooks, or any other program). The first question they ask is whether you've applied all the latest updates. If the answer is no, then they say to go apply those and call back.

You do the same with your clients. It's amazing how many issues simply go away (or never appear in the first place) when you have all the patches, fixes, and updates installed.

Just do it.

And what about **Service Packs**? Well, those do make us a little nervous. But not too bad.

I'm old enough to remember NT 4.0, Service Pack 6a. How much does it suck to have the latest Service Pack for that O.S. be a re-release of the service pack with a minor fix? It's a huge flag that says, "Let others try it first."

Microsoft has flip-flopped about service packs. In the first place, they were intended to be a collection of all the patches, fixes, and updates

Copyright © 2014 Karl W. Palachuk

for the operating system or software. But then they went through a phase of adding serious functionality. Then they removed some functionality due to lawsuits. Then they went back to only providing updates. Then they made a few exceptions to that.

Then, they invented the "roll up" so that the latest version of NT 4.0 is not SP6a, but SP6a plus the latest roll-up. (Shoot Me Now: http://support.microsoft.com/kb/299444.)

So . . . Here's our policy about these major Service Packs, Feature Packs, and Roll-ups: **Wait for about a month after they are released.** If the world does not come to an end, then schedule installs for all clients. These updates are never critical. After all, they contain mostly old patches, fixes, and updates that you've already applied. They just make it much easier to get all the latest stuff installed quickly and in an orderly manner.

Once in a great while there's a problem. But for the most part, service packs these days are uneventful. So be diligent, but don't be afraid. Give it a little time to see if there are problems, then go ahead and install.

Implementation Notes

As with all policies, you first need to spell out what you want to do with regard to software upgrades, and what your philosophy is. Write it down. Explain it to your team.

You also need to add these policies to your constant communication with clients. Put it in your newsletters. Add it to your discussions when you sell software and deliver new PCs.

Make sure everyone on your staff is promoting your vision about how software upgrades should be handled.

Copyright © 2014 Karl W. Palachuk

There are no specific forms for implementing this SOP. You might write up a brief description of the procedure and put it into your SOP binder.

This kind of policy requires that everyone on the team

1) Be aware of the policy

2) Practice the policy

3) Correct one another's errors

4) Support one another with reminders

Copyright © 2014 Karl W. Palachuk

3 and 3

Three Take-Aways from This Chapter:

1. Let clients know it's okay to skip one generation of software – but not two.

2. Always match up the hardware generation with the software generation. When they're off by more than a year or two, you have more problems.

3. Make sure everyone on your team understands and applies your policies around upgrades!!!

Three Action Steps for Your Company:

1. _____

_____

2. _____

_____

3. _____

_____

Copyright © 2014 Karl W. Palachuk

8

Nuking and Paving

There are extremely rare occasions when a computer needs to be "nuked and paved" – which is to say, completely reinstalled. Basically, a nuke and pave job is done for one of three reasons:

1. The technician is not able to fix the computer

2. There is a problem (e.g., a virus) that will take too many hours and is therefore not worth the cost

3. The problem cannot be fixed

When do you nuke and pave and when do you walk away?

Overview

The second option is completely a financial decision. If you have an old, slow PC running an old operating system, and it has a monster virus, you probably won't spend ten hours of labor trying to fix it. You shouldn't work for free, and the client doesn't want to pay $1,500 to fix a ten year old computer.

. . . unless it's the only machine in the office with a true RS-232 port and connects to their manufacturing system. Or the payroll computer the day before payroll. Or the last machine in the office that runs a critical piece of software.

Copyright © 2014 Karl W. Palachuk

Obviously you're going to do everything you can upgrade such machines, replace them, have contingencies, etc. But there just are some machines that have to be fixed, no matter what the cost.

For the average "old piece of junk" machine, however, you will nuke and pave because you can reinstall the O.S. and all software in 3-4 hours. The client might decide that they'd rather spend that 3-4 hours having you set up a new machine on the network. But, again, that's a financial decision.

It is **really** important that you have this discussion with a client before the machine dies (or is infected). It is hard to make a decision at the last minute. It's much easier if you can just look up the "Nuke and Pave Policy" for that client and refer to it.

> "Mr. Client: As we discussed six months ago, the general policy is that we will not rebuild or spend more than three hours labor fixing up the machines with Windows XP. Are you still comfortable with that decision?"

Decisions made before the disaster are often more rational and can be a good starting point when there IS a problem.

A Note on Competency

Options 1 and 3 ("The technician is not able to fix the computer" vs. "The problem cannot be fixed") can be a tough call some times. Everyone seems to think that it's easy to be a computer tech. I guess this is because everyone can use a computer.

There are some computers that just can't be fixed. But the reality is that 99% of all problems can be fixed if you have the right skills and enough time (money) to spend on the problem. In practice, I would say that most competent technicians can fix 95% of all problems.

Copyright © 2014 Karl W. Palachuk

An incompetent technician (thinks he knows a lot, but doesn't really much) can probably fix 80% of all problems. The difference is pretty huge. Incompetent technicians therefore spend a lot more time nuking and paving because it's the blunt instrument they know will fix the problem.

These folks tend to say things like "Microsoft knows this is a problem. Everyone has this problem. There's nothing we can do about it."

Let's be honest: We all start out incompetent. **Everything is difficult before it becomes easy.** But once we decide we want to do something for a living, we have an obligation to educate ourselves and take it seriously.

It hurts all of us when incompetent technicians take on tasks they can't handle. Clients become suspicious. They view our profession as one step above used car salesmen. On some days, not above.

Therefore: I think it is in your best interest to minimize the number of Nuke and Pave jobs.

Ideally, in your business, the financial calculation of #2 above will be the most important determining factor in whether you'll fix a computer. If competence is the most important factor, then you need to start tackling some tougher jobs and learn how to actually fix this stuff.

Nuke and Pave should be a last resort.

Implementation Notes

There are two policies to implement here.

First, your company should have a simple policy statement. One paragraph is good enough. It should state that your company policy is to avoid reinstalling the operating system as much as possible as a

Copyright © 2014 Karl W. Palachuk

way to "fix" problems. It should then state a simple limit on how much time you will spend on a problem. For example:

> "It the policy of our company to avoid reinstalling the operating system as much as possible as a way to fix problems. But any technician who has worked on any problem for 60 minutes without making significant progress is required to seek assistance. This assistance might be from the service manager, a vendor, or an approved back office assistance service. In any case where a desktop service ticket has consumed three or more hours of labor, the service manager will decide how we will proceed."

Second, you need to help your clients adopt similar guidelines. How much time should be spent fixing various classes of computers? In some businesses, the "classes" would be operating systems – Win8, Win7, Vista, XP, 2000, etc. In other businesses, it will be by department, such as sales, finance, etc.

Benefits

Whenever possible, the decision to nuke and pave a computer should be a **business** decision and a **financial** decision. You might really be able to fix 99% of problems instead of 95%, but if you lose money doing it, then you have to decide whether this is a hobby or a business.

As a business, you need to cut your losses. So many technicians are tempted to give away hours on long jobs. That just encourages the clients to **never upgrade** because it costs them nothing extra to keep old, crappy computers!

Eventually, this policy will help clients accept that it's cheaper in the long run to buy good equipment (and replace old equipment) than to

Copyright © 2014 Karl W. Palachuk

fix up the old stuff. The long-term effect for clients is a bunch of computers that work better, are more efficient, and keep their employees working!

The more you can make decisions based on sound financial considerations, the more money you'll make.

There are no specific forms for implementing this SOP. You might write up a brief description of the procedure and put it into your SOP or binder.

This kind of policy requires that everyone on the team

1) Be aware of the policy

2) Practice the policy

3) Correct one another's errors

4) Support one another with reminders

Copyright © 2014 Karl W. Palachuk

3 and 3

Three Take-Aways from This Chapter:

1. Set limits on how long a tech can work fruitlessly on a problem, and how many hours you will work on a machine before you Nuke and Pave.

2. Set agreements with clients about how many hours you will spend trying to fix various classes of computers in their office.

3. Don't let your ego get in the way. You don't have to fix every problem. Sometimes you have to focus on staying profitable.

Three Action Steps for Your Company:

1. _____

   _____

2. _____

   _____

3. _____

   _____

Copyright © 2014 Karl W. Palachuk

9

After Hours Work

While we like to keep it to a minimum, after hours work is a fact of life in most service businesses. As technology consultants, we need to have some guidelines about after hours work. There are lots of reasons to do this. You have costs in time and money. Your clients should have costs (because you should be charging them for the work). And if you have employees, you need to compensate them for after-hours work.

I recommend you have a statement of philosophy and a few documented policies (procedures) regarding after hours work. First the philosophy.

One of my constant arguments with technicians is about the "requirement" for after-hours work. It is only under truly extreme circumstances that you need to work after 6:00 PM on regular business days. That is a fact.

But all too often, we get into this business assuming that we need to work after hours. I can't count how many times I've been in a meeting when someone made the casual comment that "of course" you need to work after hours.

No. You choose to work after hours.

Really.

Copyright © 2014 Karl W. Palachuk

No matter how loudly you protest, it is simply a fact that *most* companies never have people work after hours – even in service businesses. Even in I.T. shops.

We have a tendency to concoct emergencies and then work after hours. Very often, these so-called emergencies simply amount to an urgent need to get something done and an unwillingness to figure out how to do it during business hours.

If you examine your after-hours labor, it is overwhelmingly normal, straight-forward tech support. It is not rebuilding a crashed server or fixing the machine needed for payroll the night before payroll is due. No, it is more likely to be just plain tech support that you felt somehow obligated to perform after hours.

I know that you don't have to work after hours because so many companies have figured out how to avoid it. You can too.

On many occasions I have challenged technicians to set up the first policy we discuss below. And guess what? 95% of their after-hours work simply disappeared. Gone. It becomes a non-issue immediately.

I encourage you to implement the same.

So the statement of philosophy goes something like this:

> Our work day is 8:00 AM to 5:00 PM Monday through Friday. Employees must receive prior authorization to work past 5:00 PM. Our clients are aware of this policy and know that after-hours work is billable at a higher rate.

Copyright © 2014 Karl W. Palachuk

Policy 1: After Hours Rates

Now for the big policy that will make your life easier. This policy has wide-reaching implications. And yet it is very simple:

Regular business hours are 8:00 AM to 5:00 PM Monday through Friday. All labor outside these hours is billable at 1.5x the regular hourly rate. This includes evenings and weekends. "All labor" includes labor on managed service agreements.

In other words, all labor covered under a managed service agreement must be between 8:00 AM to 5:00 PM Monday through Friday. Even labor that would be covered under an MSA is billable at 1.5x the regular rate if it is performed during evening or weekend hours.

(Note: We prefer to use 2x the regular rate. We get even fewer requests for after-hours with that rate.)

Implementation: Client Permission

You implement this policy by placing it in all of your service agreements. It is very reasonable and you will get no argument from clients. They may not be happy on the day they ask you to work late, but they will be very cooperative on the day they sign the agreement.

You need to have a very clear policy with your employees: If you are still working on a task at 4:30 PM, and you think you will not finish by 5:00 PM, you must contact the service manager and ask how to proceed.

In general, this is how you proceed: First, determine whether the technician is able and willing to work after 5:00 PM. If not, you need to determine whether someone else is willing to do this work. (Anyone else includes you, the owner.)

Copyright © 2014 Karl W. Palachuk

Second, you need to talk to the client. Inform him that work may be needed at 5:00 PM. Any such work would be billed at the after-hours rate. Tell the client this rate. For example, if your regular rate is $120/hour, you need to make sure the client understands that the after-hours rate is $180/hour.

If possible, give the client an estimate of the time required and ask whether they want the work done after hours or whether you should start up again in the morning.

Our experience is that clients overwhelmingly say that the work may be completed in the morning.

Note that this applies to all work – whether remote or onsite.

Implementation: Your PSA

You need to create a work type and labor rate in your PSA specifically for after-hours labor. When you are working a ticket, you need to make sure that you stop putting time on the regular agreement (managed service or time and materials) and start allocating time to the after-hours rate.

The precise process varies with your PSA. But the habit of allocating time properly is the same.

Policy 2: Onsite Access After Hours

If after hours onsite work is requested, inform the client that there must be someone from the client's company available to get your technician in and out of the building and office as needed. In addition, someone from the client's company must be present at all times in the office while your technician is on site.

Copyright © 2014 Karl W. Palachuk

This limits your liability in case that happens to be the night when something goes missing or something get broken. In addition, this will probably cost the client extra money. Therefore, it is a further deterrent to after-hours work.

A Few Comments

I am not sure why so many of us have convinced ourselves that it's "bad service" to refuse to work after hours, or to charge extra for it. Try to get an electrician to your house at 6 PM. Or an attorney. Or a plumber. Or an accountant. In most cases you'll hear that after hours appointments are simply not an option. Period. When they are available, you can bet the price will be at least 1.5x normal.

It is perfectly acceptable, and reasonable, and normal to limit your hours to "normal" work hours.

On a very personal level, you need to have a life outside work. You need to balance work and play. If you have a family, you need to tend to them. The work will really always be there. Balance and perspective will help you to see that years of working until nine or ten o'clock at night will never make the work go away. You will never get caught up. You will only lose contact with a very important (non-work) portion of your life.

One entrepreneurial approach to labor boils down to this: If you are willing to pay me enough money, I will work for you. How much I'm willing to take to sell you my time varies. There is also a limit on your willingness to pay me. So it is very natural that we come to an agreement on terms for trading dollars and hours.

Copyright © 2014 Karl W. Palachuk

3 and 3

Three Take-Aways from This Chapter:

1. Set a high rate for after-hours work and put it in all your contracts and materials.

2. Do not be afraid. You will not lose clients over this. You will make more money. And you will have more free time.

3. If you do not have a "life" or do not wish to go home, you need to fix that problem. Working all the time won't fix it.

Three Action Steps for Your Company:

1. _____

_____

2. _____

_____

3. _____

_____

Copyright © 2014 Karl W. Palachuk

10

On Call and Night Staff

Disclaimer: I'm not an employment attorney. I'm not any other kind of attorney. I only have enough common sense to know what we do in our business. You need to verify all employment policies with your attorney.

Paying Employees to Be On Call

When you grow from one to many, one of the rewards is that you - the owner - no longer have to be the only person "On Call" twenty four hours a day. You get to go on vacation because someone else is handling the details.

You also get to sleep without a cell phone next to your bed because someone else is going to get that call!

There are three primary kinds of "on call" statuses. There are different rules for each.

1. An employee is off the clock but can't go anywhere. For example, if someone has to stay in the office during their lunch hour to cover the phones or fill in for the front desk, you need to pay that person for the time. Basically, they are not free to do what they want. They have to stay there to do your bidding. Similarly, if you send a

Copyright © 2014 Karl W. Palachuk

tech to a client's office. Once they arrive, their "commute" is over and they need to be paid – even if the client is not there. Again, if the employee can't go do his own thing, then you need to pay him.

2. Employees are not at work, not scheduled to be called in, but are on the list of people who could be called in. This is aside from the fact that, really, anyone in the company could be asked to come in. Sometimes you specifically say that Person A is scheduled to work and Person B is on call in case we get busy. If Person B cannot go out of town on a whim or go drinking in the afternoon because he might have to work, then you have limited his personal time.

3. Employees who are scheduled to catch calls after hours. Just like working through lunch, these folks may never actually get a call. But they have to carry their cell phone, respond to alerts, and be ready to remote into client machines and fix things. If there is an after-hours emergency, these folks will do the after-hours work and client call-down discussed in Volume Four.

We used to call this **beeper pay**. Now the term is **sleeper pay**. But unless you're paying someone to sleep at your office, you might not have to pay them at all.

Note that #1 is pretty clear. These folks just can't go anywhere except where you need them to be. You need to pay them for that. Period.

Examples #2 and #3 are a little less clear. There's really a scale from almost-zero chance of having to work to 50% or 60% chance of having to work. In most cases, after-hours on call duty is pretty close to zero. But if they do get a call, they need to be able to respond, so they

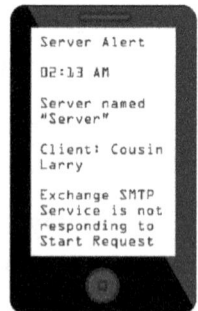

can't be otherwise engaged. Again, where on that sliding scale have you limited their freedom?

Part of this is just plain **fairness**. And part of it bumps into the laws of your state. Very often, there are no clear rules. But also very often, there are decisions by judges that become standards for other judges to use when they make decisions.

Now, just to keep it complicated, simply requiring someone to be reachable by phone is NOT considered to be restricting enough to require pay. So if you don't say anything about limiting activities (e.g., drinking) or travel, then simply being available by phone is not required to be a paid event.

If you don't have an RMM that can send out an alert, then you may have to require someone to check the service board once an hour. Now we're back into the scale discussion. How much does this limit their time, especially when no work comes in?

As a general rule, the U.S. Fair Labor Standards Act does not require that "exempt" or salaried employees be compensated for on-call duty. Thus the entire discussion applies to only hourly employees. (For a good time, check out www.dol.gov/compliance/laws/comp-flsa.htm.)

[Insert here your favorite "why people hate lawyers" joke or comment.]

Practical Recommendations

Enough speculation and legalese. Here's some practical advice to consider when you formulate your after-hours on call policy.

First, **let fairness be your guide**. Be reasonable with your employees and they will be reasonable with you. This is particularly true if your company is very small. The last thing you need is some smoldering

Copyright © 2014 Karl W. Palachuk

resentment because someone once had to work an hour in the middle of the night.

Second, if feasible, you should **rotate after hours and on call assignments** among managers and other salaried employees. Assuming that you really get very few after-hours calls or alerts, this is just a very minor limitation and very reasonable for their slightly-higher compensation. Note that the rest of the suggestions here will help make this even less of an annoyance.

Third, for hourly employees, **set a reasonable compensation**. For example, pay them time and a half for any hours outside their regular work hours. And pay a minimum of one hour or two hours for work that actually has to be done.

Fourth, set **a long response time** in your service agreement. For example, if you have a three hour response time, then your employee has lots of freedom. In three hours your employee can finish watching a kid's soccer game, drive back from the lake, or even sober up if need be.

And remember that "responding" to an alert might not really require any work. If the employee just has to acknowledge the ticket and assign it to the team at your outsourced back-office tech support, that's a three minute task. It's only when they have to sit down at their computer and log into a client machine, or drive to the client office, that serious labor takes place.

Fifth, consider a **response time in Business Hours**. That's what we do. If you say you'll respond within three business hours, then a call at 6:01 PM does not need to be acknowledged until 11:01 AM the next day. (Of course you'll respond at 8:05 AM.) This eliminates after hours on call work altogether.

Copyright © 2014 Karl W. Palachuk

You might not be comfortable with that, but you can get used to it. As I've said before, 99% of the after-hours work you do is because you've decided to do it, not because you really have to.

We have used a business hours response time policy since about 2005. It has never been an issue. We've had a few incidents in which someone has sent nagging emails and voice mails until we called them back. Then we mention that our after-hours rate is $300/hr. See the last chapter. Too bad we don't charge a "pissing me off by bugging me after hours" fee.

Sixth, if you have hourly employees on call, give them some minimal **reward for being on call** even if there are no calls. This could be a $25 gift card or something similar. You don't have to think of this as "pay" but more of a token of appreciation. This can go a long way to let employees know that you acknowledge their contribution even if they don't get an hour's pay.

Seventh (and I'm sorry about this), write up your very reasonable, well-thought-out policy and **have it reviewed by a lawyer**. She will make a minor change even if it's perfect because she has to earn her money. But once she blesses it, you're good to go.

I know a lot of this is a pain in the neck. But it is definitely worth the time and effort. After all, once you have a good workable policy, you'll be able to sleep at night without your phone on!

Copyright © 2014 Karl W. Palachuk

3 and 3

Three Take-Aways from This Chapter:

1. Create a simple after-hours on-call monitoring policy that works within the culture of your company.

2. Place a premium on fairness to your employees and they will perform excellently.

3. Consider measuring your response time in "business hours" – except for true Priority One emergencies.

Three Action Steps for Your Company:

1. _____

   _____

2. _____

   _____

3. _____

   _____

11

Managing Internal Administrative Tasks

Our organizations are outward-facing. That is, we are designed to provide services to other companies. As a result, we focus heavily on service requests from clients. But there are plenty of things to be done internally for our own companies. There are four basic types of internal activities:

- Training

- Administrative work

- Internal tech support

- "Unbillable" work done in support of managed service contracts (including drive time if you don't charge for that)

We will refer to these internal activities as "Tasks" to keep them distinct from client-facing Service Requests. You may choose to create internal Service Requests or Tasks in your PSA system. In either case, we'll refer to these internal tasks as Tasks.

We create these Tasks because we need to track all time during business hours. Why? First, we use our PSA to track employee time and generate payroll. Even though we might not be able to bill a client, we still need to pay the employee. Second, when it's time to

Copyright © 2014 Karl W. Palachuk

analyze where our time goes, we will only be able to generate meaningful reports if we put useful data into the system.

For example . . .

- It is very useful to know how many hours are spent supporting clients. This is much more than the number of "billable" hours. If you don't charge for drive time, then you need to know how much time was spent on this activity. When you have someone check the service board and verify that everything is right, that's company-wide overhead that you don't bill to a specific client. (See "Massaging the Service Board" in Volume Four of this series.)

  Note: This is not the same as labor that is included within a specific client's Managed Service Agreement. Those are Service Tickets or Service Requests and have hours allocated, but simply have a zero dollar amount.

- Internal tech support is simply the maintenance of your in-house computers and network. It's not zero. It shouldn't be too high either. If you have some technician who claims to spend an hour a day on internal tech support, you have a problem.

As with Service Requests, internal Tasks have priorities. Here's a place to start defining these:

High Priority

> Should be completed today before anything else. Must be completed before close of business. Example: Get your Supervisor Evaluation form from last week completed and turned in.

Medium Priority

Needs to be done this week or the deadline is less than a week away.

Example: Get signed up for next week's Exchange training before all spots close.

Low Priority

Needs to be done but there is no specific deadline. Usually these items are more of a reminder.

Example: Clean up your desk area.

Activity Work Flow

Activities in the PSA system are basically the "To Do" List for a technician. Activities do not violate the rule that all work is performed against a Service Request because the time will always be logged against some SR even if it is a Tech Admin SR.

An Activity with a properly assigned priority is a way for the Service Manager or a Technician to create a time slot to get a good deal of work done in a block. This avoids working in an "interrupt driven" mode. In other words, a tech can knock out six or eight little chores in a half hour block. This is far more efficient than doing each item individually between client-facing service requests. That almost always results in six or eight time entries at fifteen minutes each!

Activities are worked from highest priority to lowest and from oldest to newest.

As hard as this is to believe for some people, every task that needs to be done should be entered into your PSA system. It might be high, medium, or low priority. You have to believe in the system! If it's IN the system, it will get done. If it's not in the system, it might get done. There's a big difference between "will" and "might."

Copyright © 2014 Karl W. Palachuk

Note: You can avoid abuse by having all technicians work in real time (see Chapter Four), and by having the service manager receive emails or text messages whenever a task or service request is closed. "Real time" means that technicians enter their notes and close tickets as they complete them. There should be a steady flow of work throughout the day. If you have technicians who clock in and spend the first hour of every day on "administrative" tasks such as checking email, you give them guidance on how you would like them to work.

Implementation

This SOP requires three things. First, you need to define your priorities. Start with what we have here, but customize it for your business. Second, Write up your procedure so that you present them to technicians (and the whole staff). Third, you need to train all employees subject to this process. After that, everyone on the team should remind and support one another on this process.

There are no specific forms for implementing this SOP. You simply begin using your PSA system a bit more (or differently) than had before.

Copyright © 2014 Karl W. Palachuk

3 and 3

Three Take-Aways from This Chapter:

1. Activities are worked from highest priority to lowest and from oldest to newest.

2. Think of internal tasks very much like client service requests. But make sure you have a process to get them done.

3. Remind all technicians that they need to work in real time, whether for internal purposes or for clients.

Three Action Steps for Your Company:

1. _____

   _____

2. _____

   _____

3. _____

   _____

Copyright © 2014 Karl W. Palachuk

12

Assign Techs or Rotate Them?

There are two main schools of thought about the relationship between your technicians and your clients. One says that clients like to have a main tech they can count on, get to know, and feel comfortable with. The other says that rotating all techs between all clients provides overall better service in the long run.

There are plenty of side issues and consequences to the approach you adopt. Let's look at some of them.

Let me start off by saying that you need to talk to your clients and understand what they want before you assume that you know what they want. **Don't have both sides of the conversation.** Even if clients have an opinion, probe to determine how strongly held it is.

We sometimes assume that clients want something they have never asked for.

Example One: Sometimes we try to save the client money and we sell "cheaper" products even if they haven't asked for them.

Example Two: We frequently assume that every client request is high priority – especially if they call after hours.

Example Three: We sometimes assume that clients want super-personalized support so they're comfortable with an assigned, regularly scheduled technician.

Copyright © 2014 Karl W. Palachuk

Those things might be true sometimes for some clients. But they are usually not true for most clients.

Assigning Technicians to Clients

I think the concept of assigning specific technicians to specific clients overflows from the world of *Account Management.* Account managers are used by larger firms to handle the entire client relationship, especially for larger clients. Account managers ride herd over the service department to make sure the client is happy. They meet regularly with the client to make sure all their needs are met. And they keep an eye out for all sales opportunities to make sure the client gets quotes in a timely manner.

In smaller firms, most or all of these duties are performed by the owner or service manager of the I.T. company. As you grow, it's tempting to hand some of these duties off to the salesman or the tech.

I have heard clients complain about companies that treat them like strangers. We just acquired a new client whose primary complaint about the old service provider was that they'd been with them for five years and no one knows who they are when they call. Neither company is very large, so there's just no excuse for that.

Experiences like this lead I.T. companies to assign techs. That way the tech gets to know the machines, the people, the configurations, and the quirky stuff within the network. And, to be honest, the quirky stuff within the personal relationships at that office.

Small business clients want to feel like they've got a relationship with their service providers. If you've got technicians with good people skills, assigning technicians to clients can really help keep that relationship strong.

Copyright © 2014 Karl W. Palachuk

The downside to assigning techs should also be taken seriously. Almost every time I've heard about a technician leaving a company and trying to take clients with them, it was made possible because the technician was assigned to the client and had a strong relationship with them. Even if the technician was incompetent and not taking good care of their network, they know, like, and trust him.

One of the great dangers of having an assigned tech is that there's far less oversight of the quality of service your company is providing. See the discussion below on helping each other implement policies and processes. Remember: The consistency of your service delivery is your **brand**.

Rotating Technicians Among Clients

Let me just say that my very strong preference is to rotate all technicians through all clients.

The most important reason for this is to increase the overall quality of service provided to the client.

One of the most important reasons to adopt Standard Operating Procedures is to provide consist high quality support to your clients. One of the biggest challenges to adopting Standard Operating Procedures is that team members in isolation tend to ignore or forget SOPs. That's why lots of SOPs include the appeal to "support each other" in this policy.

As a team, you can check each other's work, verify that processes are being followed, and help each other with best practices. In isolation from the team, individual techs will virtually always stray from the chosen path. That means they will provide a lower level of service than they would if they knew other team members would see their work.

Copyright © 2014 Karl W. Palachuk

Here are some common examples:

1) An assigned tech doesn't have to complete the entire monthly maintenance if he runs out of time. He'll "get it next month" and no one will know.

2) Changes are made on the fly and not documented because the tech knows the network so well.

3) Lots of work is done without a service ticket, or inside another service ticket. No one's looking and no one will know.

4) Paperwork for hardware, software, and warranties is stuffed in a file drawer disorganized. No one's looking.

It's not like we all sit around spying on each other. But when we all know all the procedures, it's easy to help each other follow the procedures. And when a technician knows that anyone on the team could be the next person to visit a client, they take the extra two minutes to do the job right.

Don't forget another advantage to having a team: When it's time to troubleshoot or strategize about network issues, a "different pair of eyes" can be extremely helpful. The more another technician knows about the client network, the more helpful they can be.

Managing the Overall Relationship with The Client

There are just a few key elements to maintaining a good client relationship. You need to provide good service. You need to understand their needs and where their company is headed. The Roadmap meetings will help with this. And your client has to have faith that you are taking care of them.

Part of that faith comes from personal relationships. And part of it comes from the way your company presents itself. In my opinion,

Copyright © 2014 Karl W. Palachuk

having more than one technician show up at a client's office shows them that you are all cross-trained and anyone can take care of anything. It shows that you are a "shop" and not a one-person show.

On rare occasions you might have a technician who is not a good fit with a client. You may even get a note that says "We don't want him here anymore." If you get several of these, it's time to evaluate that tech's performance overall.

For the most part, having everyone on your team know everyone on the client's team makes it much easier and more comfortable to do business. No matter who is on vacation (in either company), you can work well together. And when there's turnover (in either company), the relationship continues strong.

You need to decide how your company will handle client relationships. You certainly don't have to do what we do. But you should make a conscious decision about the policy you adopt. Don't continue doing what you did yesterday just because you did it yesterday.

Copyright © 2014 Karl W. Palachuk

3 and 3

Three Take-Aways from This Chapter:

1. You need to talk to your clients and understand what they want before you assume that you know what they want.

2. Remember: The consistency of your service delivery is your brand.

3. Having everyone on your team know everyone on the client's team makes it much easier and more comfortable to do business..

Three Action Steps for Your Company:

1. _____

_____

2. _____

_____

3. _____

_____

Copyright © 2014 Karl W. Palachuk

13

Approved Tools

Many people have a "wild west" view of the tools they use in their business. Their approach amounts to this: Hire good people and let them do their thing. That sounds great, but it has a few problems. I think it's much better to have a list of "Approved Tools" that are used in your business.

Overview

There is one very strong argument to be made for having an approved set of tools (software programs) that you use in your company: **Standardization** means higher profit, more predictability, and fewer problems.

The primary arguments against having a standard, well-defined set of tools are:

1) You might not have "the best" tool
   on your list

and

2) Things change fast, so the best tool
   might change, and then you won't be
   using it

Copyright © 2014 Karl W. Palachuk

Basically, these arguments represent fear that there's some "better" thing out there and you should be using it. Fine. You should have a process for evaluating and adding tools to your list. But you cannot simply let technicians use whatever they want.

The primary problem with letting technicians do whatever they want are:

1) You cannot reproduce the work. That means you can't properly troubleshoot if you don't know which tools are used. You can replicate problems. You can't replicate **success**!

2) The Internet is filled with spyware, viruses, and a LOT of really crappy, poorly-written homemade tools that you can download for free. Thanks to the wonders of modern programming, almost anyone can write a poorly behaved software program that can cripple a server by accident.

Approved tools means that you have some kind of a process for determining when a tool can be used in your business. For example, the most common kinds of tools on your "approved" list will be:

- Any tool distributed by Microsoft

- Any tool distributed by your preferred Anti-Virus vendor

- Tools you've purchased or licensed

- Services you subscribe to

For many years we have preferred the tools and "widgets" distributed by Microsoft. Even if they come with a warning that they're not supported, we believe they are vetted in large part by wide-spread usage. Robocopy is an example of such a tool.

Copyright © 2014 Karl W. Palachuk

What you **don't want** is for a technician to Google something, download whatever looks good, install it on a client network, and destroy the client's system. Obviously, that's the worst case scenario.

Much more commonly, an old or poorly-written tool can replace a key .dll and cause problems that lie dormant and are difficult to trace.

Many legitimate tools are also troublesome. For example, we used to use Belarc advisor many years ago. But their licensing is very clear that it is not intended for consultants to install wherever they want and make money without paying anything to Belarc. That's why they have a professional subscription.

More importantly, we have RMM agents on all of our client machines. So there's no reason for a technician to install something else. Belarc reports don't draw data from our RMM, provide data to our RMM, or provide us with key information that's not already in our RMM. So there's no point in installing one more program to get data we're already getting. The tech should learn and use the approved tool.

Another minor argument for letting techs use whatever tool they want is that they will use tools they know well and are comfortable with, so they will work faster. Maybe. In reality, this is often a license to go fishing on the Internet to find something new and cool. The first choice should be an approved tool.

Here's another example: There are a hundred places you could go to look up Event ID notices and what they mean. The "easiest" is simply Google. But with Google, the tech is likely to wander down several rabbit holes before he finds the right answer. And now that Google indexes every tech support forum on earth, your technician will likely read hundreds of posts that simply say "Yeah, I have the same problem."

Copyright © 2014 Karl W. Palachuk

If you have an approved tool such as EventID.net, the tech is much more likely to spend time on task and solve the problem quickly.

Benefits and Notes

As with most SOPs, the goal is to increase overall success as a TEAM. That means that you can go from machine to machine, client to client, and know that you won't run into a different set of minor issues with each computer because of the hodge-podge of tools being used.

Consistency.

Reproducibility.

Reliability.

Note, please, that you don't need a long list here. In fact, you need a short list. What do you use for . . .

- Anti-Virus
- Special virus fix-ups
- Hard drive recovery
- Registry maintenance
- Password locker
- File maintenance and sizing
- ISO imaging
- Screen captures
- FTP/TFTP
- System Information
- Patch Management

Copyright © 2014 Karl W. Palachuk

- Remote Access

These probably cover 95% of all issues you deal with. It may not make sense to have standardized tools for other things because you will use them so seldom. And, depending on what you do on a daily basis, you might not need all of these.

This SOP is not implemented with forms, but with a software directory. Whether on SharePoint, a cloud storage area, or on your own server via a mapped drive, you should have a directory that contains your tools. For items with installable files and license keys, you'll create sub-directories.

This policy is implemented with a brief memo outlining the approved tools and where they're stored.

As with all other policies, it's important that members of the team help to remind each other of the policy, and to implement it.

Copyright © 2014 Karl W. Palachuk

3 and 3

Three Take-Aways from This Chapter:

1. Define one or two tools that are the first choices for technicians to use during a virus/spyware cleanup.

2. You should have a process for evaluating and adding tools to your list of approved tools.

3. You need to have a balance between using known, good tools and being open to new tools that are necessary in response to the quick-changing world of technology.

Three Action Steps for Your Company:

1. _____

_____

2. _____

_____

3. _____

_____

Copyright © 2014 Karl W. Palachuk

14

Do Not Exclude Yourself from the Rules

We all know that SOPs – Standard Operating Procedures – make your business run better. We all know that we need to train our employees to document procedures, learn procedures, and follow procedures. But all too often, the bosses and owners don't follow the rules we set for our companies.

When we start a new business, we have to do everything ourselves. There aren't many procedures. Procedures evolve over time. And even then, we shortcut the procedures whenever we're in a hurry. It's a natural evolution.

Once employees come along, three important things change for the business owner. First, "I" becomes "We." Second, the owner becomes a team leader. Third, the owner spends a good deal of time getting in the way of her employees.

It can take a long time to build a business up from one person to

Rules

1. *Always carry a dime in case you need to call a cab*
2. *Turn off the lights when you leave the room*
3. *Wear your seatbelt*
4. *Never run with scissors*
5. *Always wear clean underwear*
6. *Be kind to animals*
7. *For that matter, be kind to people as well*
8. *Don't eat other peoples' lunches from the fridge*
9. *Pay your bills*
10. *Save for retirement*
11. *Visit your grandmother*
12. *. . . and your parents when they're old*
13. *Hire good people and let them do their jobs*
14. *Don't be "cheap"*
15. *Do unto others as you would have them do unto you. Seriously.*
16. *Teach your children well*
17. *Lend a helping hand to strangers*
18. *Neither a borrower nor a lender be*
19. *All work must be done from a remote reposit*
20. *Replace your hardware every three years*

several. The owner has a tendency to think of the company as himself. After all:

- I built this company

- I decided when to cut left or right

- I got us here

- It's my company

But when you start hiring employees, "I" no longer does all the work: We do the work. Eventually, the owner hands off some tasks and knows that he'll never do them again. At first, you have to consciously try to remember to use the Royal We. But this becomes easier over time.

Part of the process of being "We" is that you get in the habit of describing your company and your services in those terms. For example, "We like to get a full backup before we start a server migration." That's not just one person's good habit. That's what the company does and that's what the client can expect. Many of your best practices can be projected to the clients in this manner.

The owner becomes a team leader automatically with the first employee. But once you have solid SOPs in place, it's the owner's constant responsibility to build up the SOPs as part of the company brand. This is the way we do things. This is what makes us different. This is what makes us who we are.

If team leader isn't blunt enough for you, let me put it another way: The owner becomes the enforcer. Assuming you have good processes, the more consistently you enforce your processes, the stronger your brand becomes.

Copyright © 2014 Karl W. Palachuk

When everyone does whatever they want, you don't really have a business. You have a bunch of people working together to try to make money. And that's fine. But if you want a business, you need to have consistently reproducible results. To make that happen the owner must become the enforcer of SOPs.

The first real job I had was in a hardware store. I remember both the owner and the store manager used to tell me: "When you have your own store you can do whatever you want. When you work here, you do things our way." And so it is in your business.

Eventually, the business is mature enough to have several employees and several SOPs that are employed consistently. One of the very natural pieces of evolution is that the owner becomes the choke point. Marketing decisions have to be approved by the owner. Office supply purchases have to be approved by the owner. Time cards have to be approved by the owner.

The owner has started to delegate but is still the ultimate decision maker for all important decisions.

Only when you break past this barrier can your business move to the next level. Either you stagnate, or break the limit. It could go either way. With luck, you learn the next level of delegation and learn to delegate authority and not just tasks. When you delegate authority there's no limit to how large your business can grow.

At this point it is very clear why the owner (and now the managers) must obey the SOPs of the organization. That means that you use the ticketing system just as you expect your technicians to do. That means you follow the process for turning in mileage reports, just like everyone else. That means you follow the rules just like everyone else.

When you have a mature operation that runs smoothly, you can really muck things up when you exclude yourself from the rules. First, you can actually make a mess. For example, if you just grab the phone and start answering client questions, you've short-circuited the service delivery process. The service manager and service coordinator don't know what you're up to and you don't know about the other problems or the context of the issue you're working on. Whether they tell you or not, they're mumbling that you should stay out of the service department.

Second, this can lead to bad morale within your company. Watching the boss is a favorite past time. When the boss doesn't follow the rules, everyone notices. Employees will mumble, "Notice that we have to track time in real time but he doesn't" (and many similar complaints.) And they will be justified to notice this.

You are building these SOPs for good reasons. Please follow them. Take them as seriously as you want your employees to take them. And more importantly, just get in the habit of doing this as your company evolves. That will make it easier.

It is a very natural tendency to say "I own this place, I'm the boss, and I can do whatever I want." But that attitude will cost your company money and keep you from reaching its greatest potential.

3 and 3

Three Take-Aways from This Chapter:

1. Ask your team to remind you to follow the process. This can be done nicely and with humor.

2. "Live" inside the PSA all day long. This will help you stay tuned into the processes your company uses.

3. When you do billable labor or move the sales process forward, enter time in the PSA and update statuses appropriately. Be a perfect example for your staff.

Three Action Steps for Your Company:

1. _____

_____

2. _____

_____

3. _____

_____

Copyright © 2014 Karl W. Palachuk

Copyright © 2014 Karl W. Palachuk

15

When Policies and Procedures Become Obsolete

From time to time, policies and procedures become obsolete. So ... of course ... there has to be a standard operating procedure for "decommissioning" policies and procedures.

Changing Procedures More Frequently

In Volume One, Chapter One we defined the difference between policies and procedures. Basically, policies are more permanent than procedures, although both will change.

Given the different nature of procedures vs. policies, you will change procedures much more frequently. For example, your checklists for new servers and new desktops are likely to change at least once a year. Changes to service packs, hardware choices, and software versions may require these procedures to be updated more frequently than that.

In a perfect world, policies will change very rarely. But changes will happen.

Copyright © 2014 Karl W. Palachuk

Three Places to Record Changes

When Policies and Procedures become obsolete, you will need to make changes in three places: Paper records, your PSA, and your electronic files.

Paper records may exist in your SOP binder, in client Network Documentation Binders, and in various places around your office (such as pinned to a bulletin board). But don't freak out. That's about it. Your policies and procedures should not be scattered all over the place in paper format.

Depending on how automated you are, you may not have anything in paper format. But I doubt that you're 100% paperless.

It is very important that you do not destroy old written paper documentation - especially if it includes client-specific information such as IP addresses, passwords, ISP configurations, etc. Instead, draw a single line across the page. Do not scratch out the information so it is unreadable. Just one line, so you can read the old information.

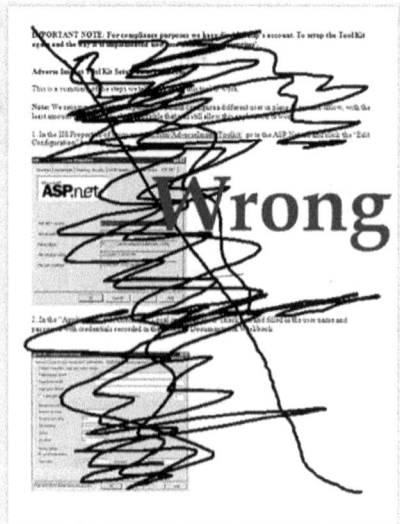

You literally never know when you will need old information. Ghosts from the past show up when you least expect it.

After you cross out the page, simply place it in the back of the appropriate section of the SOP binder or Network Documentation Binder.

Documentation in your PSA is treated pretty much the same. In this case, however, you simply rename the procedure with the prefix "!Old" or "!Retired". (The ! is there simply to be consist with the next subject: Your electronic files.)

In some PSA systems, you can move obsolete configurations and procedures to a subfolder or some other place so that they are away from the main area where you look for current information. In some you can mark items as "inactive" or some other status so that they do not show up unless you are specifically looking for them.

Your Electronic Files should be stored in a logical, usable location. See Volume Two, Chapter 67 on "Organizing Your Company Files and Folders."

Notice that one of the categories there is \Operations\Processes and Procedures. Well, within that, you will eventually need to rename files so that it's clear they are no longer in use. For example, you might replace the file "Phone Tree Text.docx" with an updated version.

Best practice is to rename the old file and not delete it. You might rename such files with !Old or !Obsolete. For example, "!Old Phone Tree Text.docx". Or your could create a directory such as \Operations\Processes and Procedures\!Old and put all retired items there.

I hope you see the big pattern here: Never throw away any old policies, processes, or procedures. Yes, the world changes. Things

Copyright © 2014 Karl W. Palachuk

grow old. Policies evolve. Processes change. So you need to make sure you have a process for keeping that stuff – but keeping out it out of sight.

Someone will ask for an example of why we need old information. Here's a perfect example: The client changed ISPs and moved email from the old ISP to in-house Exchange server. A year later, they need to open the PST file for a former employee. But it is saved with the password used at the old ISP.

If you have that old password list, you can simply open the file. If not, you have to find a program to crack the password . . . and pass those costs on to your client.

As always, you don't have to use the same process we use, but you should have some standard procedure for dealing with obsolete policies and procedures. The most important thing is to never lost old information because you don't know when you might need it. Once you accept that, you simply have to figure out HOW you're going to keep track of the old documentation.

3 and 3

Three Take-Aways from This Chapter:

1. Never throw anything away. You can rename it, archive it, or hide. But don't delete it. Ever. Really.

2. When you retire a printed document, draw one line through each page. Do not cross out or mess up the documentation.

3. Determine *your* standards for naming/renaming files. Write a memo and then make sure everyone follows the standard.

Three Action Steps for Your Company:

1. _____

   _____

2. _____

   _____

3. _____

   _____

Copyright © 2014 Karl W. Palachuk

Copyright © 2014 Karl W. Palachuk

Section II

Employees in the Tech Department

Copyright © 2014 Karl W. Palachuk

Copyright © 2014 Karl W. Palachuk

16

Technician Time Management Guidelines

This procedure covers the standard "routine" for a technician. Before you get into any details, please note one critically important thing: The point of all of this process is to . . .

Avoid being Interrupt Driven.

By "interrupt driven" I simply mean that you allow yourself to be interrupted and therefore end up doing whatever interrupted you most recently. This is so important that I've addressed it in several books and many times in my blog. It's a simple phrase and a very difficult concept to implement. Just like exercise, if you get out of the habit of non-interruption for a few days, it can take some work to get back on track.

We allow ourselves to be interrupted by the telephone. How often is the telephone call more important than what you were doing? 2% of the time? We allow Outlook to pop up and beg for our attention. Then we have to go back to work. We let instant messengers from three different channels pop up and grab our attention. We check Facebook, Twitter, and our cell phones non-stop as if the world might actually end and we'd miss it.

Copyright © 2014 Karl W. Palachuk

Enter → Begin Work Day

Check Time

Is Work Scheduled for You at This Time? (SR or Task)
- YES → Perform Scheduled Work
- NO ↓

Do You Have Email To Process?
- YES → Process Email Per Policy
- NO ↓

Any Priority 1 SR's Assigned to You?
- YES → Work P 1 Tickets
- NO ↓

Any High Priority Activities Assigned to You?
- YES → Work High Pri Activities
- NO ↓

Any Priority 2 SR's Assigned to You?
- YES → Work P 2 Tickets
- NO ↓

Any Medium Priority Activities Assigned to You?
- YES → Work Med Pri Activities
- NO ↓

Any Priority 3 SR's Assigned to You?
- YES → Work P 3 Tickets
- NO ↓

Any Low Priority Activities Assigned to You?
- YES → Work Low Pri Activities
- NO ↓

Any Priority 4 SR's Assigned to You?
- YES → Work P 4 Tickets
- NO ↓

Work on Training or Admin Tasks Until Top of the Hour
↓

Is It near end of work day?
- NO → (back to Check Time)
- YES → Begin End of Day Process → Exit

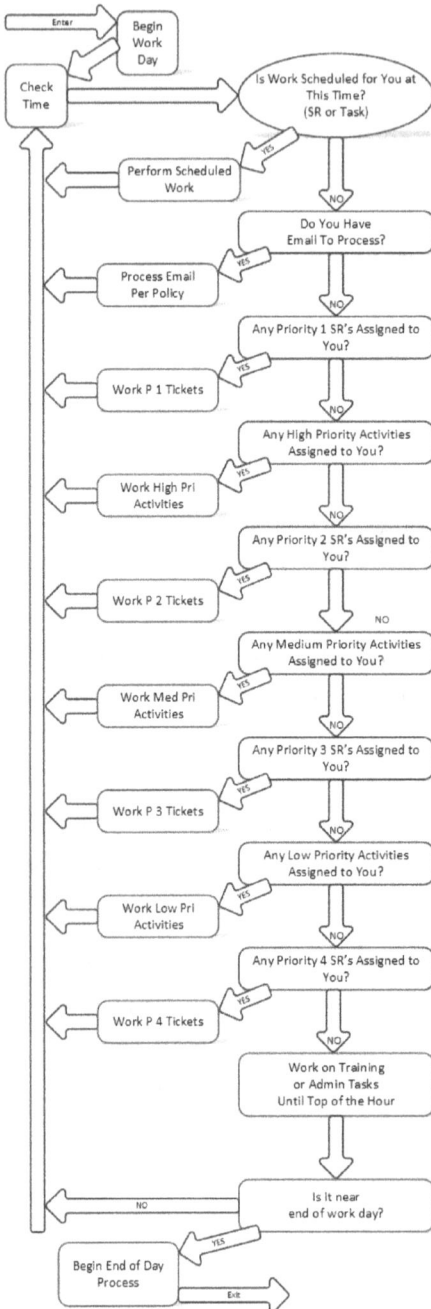

This process does not end interruptions. But it does provide a framework for getting things done based on priorities rather than "most recent interruption."

The Technician's Day

The Technician's Day is a routine and it is expected that all technicians will follow it very closely. This routine is simply a continuously looping process of subroutines. After each numbered subroutine, begin at the top of the list again. For example, if you have managed to complete the subroutine "Work P2 Tickets" you go back to the top and work your way through the subroutines in order. See the diagram.

Don't let the diagram confuse you.

The basic process is this:

1) Check the time. Remember that scheduled work always takes precedence over "regular" priority-based service tickets.

2) Check email to process. You have two options here. You can have technicians check email every time they loop through, or limit it to a few times per day. For example, if the time is 8 AM, 10 AM, 1 PM, or 3 PM, then check email. Technicians do not need to hang out in email all day. Neither does anyone else, really.

3) Check for the highest priority items that you can work on. You cycle through these in the following order: P1 Tickets, High Priority Activities, P2 Tickets, Medium Priority Activities, P3 Tickets, Low Priority Activities, and P4 Tickets.

   1. If you are very busy, it is unlikely that a technician will clear out all P1, P2, P3, and P4 tickets. If so, then you move onto

4) Other things that need to be done. This includes studying for exams, administrative work, cleaning up the office. Whatever needs to be done.

Since the entire process really amounts to beginning the day, **working everything in priority order**, and ending the day, it is easy to learn. Remember, one of our mantras is that nothing should ever be lost, dropped, or forgotten. That's why it is critical that everything be in your PSA system (Autotask, ConnectWise, TigerPaw, or whatever). Once it's in the system, and every technician is cycling through this process, you will eventually work every ticket and every task.

The Warm Up

There is a bit of process that takes place before the technician starts the day. Because a service environment is always changing, it is reasonable to expect that a technician will check email and the PSA in

Copyright © 2014 Karl W. Palachuk

the morning before heading into work (or perhaps the evening before).

The service manager might want the technician to show up at a client's office first thing in the morning. Or perhaps pick up supplies. Or whatever. The main thing you want to avoid is having the technician show up at the office and discover that he should be at a client's office instead.

In our project management, we sometimes use the "golden hour" of 7:00 AM to 8:00 AM to accomplish tasks before clients show up for work. If your technician is expected to be at a client's office (or working remote) at 7:00 AM, they need to know this before showing up for work at 8:00 AM!

Checking the service board and this bit of email are trivial tasks. They amount to "checking your work schedule" and are not paid time. Technicians are NOT expected to do anything else with the service board at this time. Technicians are NOT expected to process all of their email at this time. The only thing they need to do is figure out where to be to start the day.

Not Every Tech Can Work Every Ticket

If you have more than one technician, then you know that not every technician can work every ticket. This might be because of knowledge, skill, client relations, or whatever. In addition, some tickets will be assigned to specific technicians. So, if a tech looks at a ticket and sees that it is assigned to someone else, he should move on to the next ticket.

It is not uncommon that you will have a scenario such as this: Tom shows up for work and starts the process. He checks email and then looks at tickets. There are no P1 tickets and no high priority tasks (this is very common). He checks P2 tickets. There are five. One is assigned to Bob, one is assigned to Mike. One is waiting for client feedback. One is scheduled for Friday.

At this point, there is only one P2 ticket that Tom can work. When Tom reviews the notes, he might discover that it's a system he doesn't understand, or that it has escalated to a level beyond what he is able to do. That's fine. He moves on to Medium Priority tasks (internal "to do" items), and then on to P3 tickets.

There are two key things to remember here. First, each technician is expected to do what he can to move each ticket forward as much as possible. Part of the measure of a successful day is moving tickets through the system.

Second, you want to avoid (at all costs) the scenario in which a technician opens a ticket, looks through the notes, decides he can't make progress, logs time, and then logs out. Really good notes, and direction from the Service Manager go a long way to avoiding this scenario. Use the code WITNS ("What is the next step?") to flag the obvious next step. If the next step is to call tech support, then your technician should not begin this work fifteen minutes before the end of the day. If the next step is to deliver hardware on site, the tech can't work that from home.

Don't let techs log useless time against tickets. A good process will keep them from this is the first place.

A key piece of the service manager's job is to "massage" the service board. See Volume Four in this series. To the extent that it makes everything run more smoothly, he should also keep the technicians up to speed about what they should be doing. The formal process is a framework for success. But a little human wisdom and common sense go a long ways. Most of the time, most technicians will be working on

Copyright © 2014 Karl W. Palachuk

P3 and P4 tickets, and low priority tasks. In other words, these are not time-sensitive issues. So there is some flexibility.

For example, if a specific program needs an update across several clients, you might have a technician work all of these at P3 tickets in one sitting. The tech will be more efficient, and you'll know that the issue has been handled. The formal process has no way of "knowing" that kind of information. But people can handle this very easily!

Implementation

This procedure takes a little time to implement. First, you need to create a flow chart similar to the one posted here. It needs to make sense for your company, so make adjustments as needed. Next, you need to write up the process and how it affects technicians. Finally, you need to train the technicians and then make sure everyone is working the system.

It will take a little effort for the service manager to monitor that everyone is working from highest priority to lowest priority. It means checking in with them, watching the tickets they complete, and reminding everyone of the process. You might even print up your flow chart and have everyone post it at their workstation.

Another one of our mantras is that we work from highest priority to lowest, from oldest to newest. This process is targeted at achieving exactly that goal. If that's your goal, then this is a good place to start.

Copyright © 2014 Karl W. Palachuk

3 and 3

Three Take-Aways from This Chapter:

1. Create a "flow chart" that makes sense within your company. Train techs and hold them accountable.

2. Determine when techs should check email and then enforce it. Verify that people do not camp out in Outlook all day.

3. Working from highest priority to lowest priority, everything should move faster. How will you measure that?

Three Action Steps for Your Company:

1. _____

_____

2. _____

_____

3. _____

_____

Copyright © 2014 Karl W. Palachuk

Copyright © 2014 Karl W. Palachuk

17

Time Tracking for Employees

Tracking your time and your employees' time has two major effects on your profitability. Both of them are critical and worth serious attention.

On one hand, labor is the largest expense of any organization with one or more employees. That means you need to keep accurate track of how employees spend their time so you can keep costs under control. In addition to the total hours spent on an employee, you need to keep track of the time spent working tickets and on administrative tasks.

On the other hand, you need to keep accurate track of the labor you are able to bill to your clients. In addition, you should keep track of the mix of billable and non-billable labor spent working tickets. You need to make sure you bill for everything you should. And even for the things that are covered by a managed service agreement, you need to keep track of the total hours in order to determine whether you're being profitable.

Here are a few guidelines that might be helpful. As always, you need to adjust for the processes and procedures in place in your company.

Copyright © 2014 Karl W. Palachuk

Tracking Employee Time

We use a PSA (professional services automation) system - and recommend that you do too. If you're still not familiar with PSA systems, it is well worth your time to look into them.

We started out like most companies, tracking our own time and building a system to automate as much as possible. Then we invested in one PSA and used them for several years. Eventually, we decided that a move to another PSA made more sense for our business.

With any PSA system, tracking employee time is a key component. We have a few simple rules about employee time:

1. Employees must track all time from 8:00 am to 5:00 pm every week day

2. We created a way to track lunch breaks so that they are not part of the employee's payroll time sheet

3. Employee time is billable to us when the employee is working on client tickets, "administrative" time, or travel time. Trips to the bank or to pick up the kids from school are not covered by payroll.

4. All work is done on a service ticket. No ticket, no work. No exceptions.

5. Everyone must work in real time

Our most important rule about time tracking - and the hardest one to get some employees to follow – is that **We work in real time.** That means that you enter time into the PSA as you complete each task. Even if it's a single 15 minute time entry.

When you complete any service ticket, you enter notes into the system and put in your time. Right then and there. **You do not save them up and enter all time at once.** To make accurate time entries, you need to work in real time unless you have perfect recall or perfect notes. (Hint: you don't have these.)

I can't believe how many excuses there are for NOT putting in time as soon as the ticket is entered. They all sound a bit like this:

"I'm too busy. I don't have time. There are other, more pressing matters. I have a crisis."

All of which can be translated as:

"I'm not in the habit. I don't remember. I don't think it's important. I'm lazy. Getting the work done is important; Getting the paperwork done is not."

The mentality of technicians is such that we just want to **fix things**, not document what we did. But that documentation is important for a hundred reasons we won't go into here. One reason rules above all else: Money. When we document our work and close the ticket, we can prove that we did the job. We know what we did, when we did it, and the status of the job.

When you have even two employees, one will be managing the job board. That person needs to know the status of the jobs at a glance. That's where the PSA comes into the picture. The manager needs to be able to look at the job board at a glance and know what's going on. If the tech works a bunch of tickets and then wants to put the time in at night, the manager actually has no idea what's going on at any time.

Furthermore, if you have more than one tech, and a client who is nervous about a task, the job board is the only place for all the techs, and the manager to put notes and keep each other informed. What happens if Tech A finishes a job but keeps the notes for later tonight when he's got a beer in front of him? Tech B picks up a service ticket and begins working it. You lose money. Period.

The service manager/coordinator should be able to look at the text messages on his cell phone and see that his people are making progress. He should see a steady series of updates from the PSA as jobs enter the board and move on to completion. If his phone is silent all day and he gets 20 text messages at 8:30 PM, then his techs are not working in real time.

Building The Habit can be difficult, especially if you're a one-man shop. But it's still important. You need to know how long it really takes to do certain jobs. We all have estimates, but we can fool ourselves if we don't actually track the time. Even if you give the hours away, you need to do that consciously.

Tracking Client Time

The time we pay employees is closely related to the time we bill clients, but this is not a perfect correlation. Because we run a managed service business, we spend a good deal of time doing work that's "covered" under an MSA (managed service agreement).

In the beginning, we created our MSAs based on our estimates of how much time we actually spend maintaining servers, workstations, and network equipment. But what if we're wrong? What if one client takes twice as much time as we estimated? Are we still profitable?

Copyright © 2014 Karl W. Palachuk

Client time is divided into three primary types:

- Managed Service Labor (covered)

- Billable Labor

- Non-Billable Labor

Billable labor is then divided into regular hourly work and after-hours work. The after-hours rate is twice as much as the regular rate.

Managed Service Labor is time spent performing maintenance or (covered) repair work. Basically, if something is working and stops working, the labor to make it work again is covered.

Billable Labor refers to project or add/move/change work. This includes installing software, switching out desktops, creating new users, etc.

Non-Billable Labor is not the same as MSA labor. Non-Billable Labor is simply "billable" labor that the service manager has decided to give the client for free. For example, let's say that you estimated three hours to configure a content filtering system and it took the technician four hours. You could bill the client full price for three hours and then bill zero for the fourth hour.

That last little bit is important: You want all four hours to show up on the client's bill so they SEE that they got an hour for free. But you're sticking to your estimate of three billable hours. This subject is covered under Time Tracking for Employees because you need to make sure that all time is properly allotted.

Put it All Together - In one visit, a technician can sit down at a desktop and run a PC Tune-Up (covered work), then install a new piece of software (billable work). This should require TWO different service tickets. The first one is covered by the MSA and includes maintenance labor. When that job is done, the technician can go into the ticket, enter notes, enter time, and change the status to Completed or Closed (depending on your processes).

The second task is a separate ticket, which is attached to a billable labor (non-managed service) contract. When the job is done, the technician goes into the ticket, enters notes, enters time, and then changes the status to Completed or Closed.

This process only takes a few SECONDS to complete, unless the notes are extensive. Later, when trying to remember which job took how much time, and how the two hours should be allocated, the technician will be working with imperfect notes and imperfect recall. Will the job accurately reflect the billable time? You hope so, but you have no way of actually knowing.

Implementation Notes

As I've mentioned before, GIGO (garbage in, garbage out) applies to your PSA system. You won't be able to get accurate reports OUT of your system unless you put accurate information INTO the system. So when it's time to figure out how billable each technician is, or whether a client is profitable, you must assume that the data in your PSA system is accurate.

The data in your system will only be accurate when everyone works in real time and enters their time according to the process you've laid out.

First, you need to define your process in a simple paragraph or two.

Second, you need to train your employees. Use real world example with real clients to show them how it works.

Third, your entire team needs to support one another in this. Ask each other "Are you working in real time?" Follow the rules regarding billable and non-billable time. Massage the service board to make sure all tickets and time is properly allocated.

Fourth, force employees to follow the rules. Reject bad time cards. Make them stop what they're doing to get back into real time. Remember the long view and don't be short-sighted about what's important to your company.

Copyright © 2014 Karl W. Palachuk

3 and 3

Three Take-Aways from This Chapter:

1. Everyone in you company should be tracking time in Real Time. Even the managers. Even the owner.

2. Make sure that everyone understand the kinds of billable and non-billable labor performed.

3. Your job estimates will become more accurate as you do a better job of tracking your time in real time.

Three Action Steps for Your Company:

1. _____

   _____

2. _____

   _____

3. _____

   _____

Copyright © 2014 Karl W. Palachuk

18

The Tech on Call for The Day - Managing Daily Work Flow

There are several roles that need to be performed within the service delivery department. Obviously, there are technicians. When you get a few techs, you'll eventually have a service manager. In Volume Two we discussed Service Manager Roles and Responsibilities as well as Technician Roles and Responsibilities.

Now let's talk about the "Tech on Call for the Day" role. This discussion can also be applied to a service coordinator role. I will use the terms Service Coordinator and Tech on Call interchangeably. Notice that I'm very careful to refer to this as a role, because this role might be performed by almost anyone in the company. When you're just starting out, the owner will wear this hat along with the technician hat, service manager hat, front office hat, and all the other hats.

I like to call it the Tech on Call for the Day because that's a very good way to transition into having levels of responsibility in your service department. You can rotate this role between each of the techs on a schedule that makes sense for you. You might rotate every day or every week.

Rotating this role takes these responsibilities away from the owner or service manager, allowing that person to be more productive in higher level activities. Rotation has other benefits as well. It allows

Copyright © 2014 Karl W. Palachuk

you to "test drive" each of the techs to see how they might do with additional responsibility. And it's a great way to make sure each of the techs understands the rules of service board management, setting priorities, scheduling work, etc.

Of course you have to decide who will and who will not rotate into this position and how frequently. In the beginning, the owner or service manager will have to spend a lot of time with the Tech on Call for the Day.

The list of duties is essential to your daily procedures and as such they are to be reviewed and changed periodically in order to fit your policies better. Please do not consider this list static. In addition, be open to input from anyone who rotates into the Tech of the Day position. This will help you continue to fine-tune your processes.

Tasks to be performed by the person assuming the Service Coordinator / Tech on Call For The Day role:

a. When you are "on point" for the day, you will be monitoring the Service Board and updating it at least every hour.

b. Take over the phones. This means that you will catch incoming calls. The actual process for this will vary depending on your phone system.

Remember, the Coordinator role is there to accept new requests from clients but you are not there to answer billing or service related questions. If that happens, simply explain to the client your role is there to take down the issue and then enter it into the

Copyright © 2014 Karl W. Palachuk

system. For further questions please refer the client to management.

Also remember: This is not a "help desk" position. The Coordinator is not authorized to answer the phone and start solving the client's problem. Nothing in this position eliminates the need to enter service requests into the PSA system, prioritize them, and work them from highest to lowest priority and from oldest to newest. Tickets have to get into the system; but we are not interrupt-driven with regard to work priorities.

It is helpful to give this person a call script so they know what to say under various circumstances. Don't throw them in and hope they can swim!

c. You will be managing the outsourced monitoring and help desk (RMM / back office) and therefore need to be the designated coordinator in their system. Log into their system and make this change, or call them to notify them. In general, follow whatever process they need.

d. You are in charge of letting the remote monitoring service know when we are doing maintenance on a server that would require either downtime or reboots. Use the message board and post a message accordingly. Again, follow their process.

e. Perform the daily monitoring duties as described in "Daily Monitoring of Clients" in Volume Four of this series.

f. Process the new Service Requests that come into the system. To do this follow the guidelines established in Volume Four, Section I of this series, in particular, the following chapters:

- "Service Ticket Updates"

- "Ticket Statuses to Use and When to Use Them"

Copyright © 2014 Karl W. Palachuk

- "Setting Job Priorities"

- "Massaging the Service Board"

- "How Do Service Requests Get Into Your System?"

g. Work on Priority 4 Service Tickets. This is one way we make sure that the P4 tickets get attention. You need to be interruptible enough to take phone calls and perform all the little tasks above. Working low-priority tickets is a perfect combination as you can switch tasks fairly easily.

h. Unless the service manager has a reason to do otherwise, you will work service tickets that involve working with line-of-business tech support, shadowing them as they access client machines, and generally making their support work as successful as possible. Ideally, this work is scheduled at a specific time. And since our primary responsibility is simply to monitor the vendor's access, it fits well with the coordinator role.

i. As higher-level tickets enter the system, you will coordinate with technicians to make sure that they are working on the highest-level, oldest tickets in the queue. If technicians are scheduled to be out at client offices, you will keep track of who is where and how they will proceed through their day. Sometimes, jobs are finished faster than expected. At other times, they drag on longer than expected. The "coordinator" piece of this job is to balance all the resources (people) available to your and tickets that need attention.

In general, the Service Coordinator role will help to move tickets through the system. In a perfect world, this role would not be needed because the process of prioritizing tickets and then working them from highest to lowest priority and from oldest to newest will always

Copyright © 2014 Karl W. Palachuk

keep everyone doing exactly what they should be doing. But since you are also dealing with human beings, there is a good portion of "art" in addition to the science of managing tickets.

Implementation Notes

First, you need to define the specific duties to be performed by the Tech on Call for The Day. These will be some subset of duties already being performed by one or more people. In fact, it may include some things that should be getting done but aren't. Write out the duties in a manner similar to the list above.

Second, you need to determine a rotation schedule. Who will rotate through this role? How often will you rotate? Will the service manager or owner be on the rotation list?

Third, once you've written out the duties and rotation, you need to do some training. All the technicians should be familiar with the basic tasks required for this position. But very often, we don't pay close attention to the details of jobs that are not our own. So they might know the broad outline but not the details of performing the tasks. Training of some kind is in order.

Fourth, set a schedule and begin the rotation. Do some debriefing after one day, three days, and one week. Accept lots of feedback, give lots of feedback, and fine-tune the process in response to the realities of your business.

Benefits

The most obvious benefit is that this process is an evolutionary stage as your business moves from one-tier to a multi-level service department. It is a good way to transition to having a full-time service

Copyright © 2014 Karl W. Palachuk

coordinator, but it allows you to see how each technician will do without making permanent changes.

The rotation will also increase the efficiency of your team as each technician learns a higher level of detail about the flow of tickets through the system and the fine points of service coordination. Setting priorities, coordinating schedules, and working with clients. When everyone on the team has a higher level of understanding for these functions, they will all be better at supporting and reinforcing one another. That takes your team and your service delivery to the next level.

Copyright © 2014 Karl W. Palachuk

3 and 3

Three Take-Aways from This Chapter:

1. We often pay no attention to the details of a job that is not our own. Rotating the Coordinator position will help everyone learn these tasks.

2. The Service Coordinator is the most interruptible person on the tech team. But even they can't be *too* interruptible.

3. When you start this process, you'll need to help and monitor each tech as they learn the tasks in this role. It's harder than it looks!

Three Action Steps for Your Company:

1. _____

   _____

2. _____

   _____

3. _____

   _____

Copyright © 2014 Karl W. Palachuk

Copyright © 2014 Karl W. Palachuk

19

How to Maximize Billability of Technicians

This chapter assumes you have a ticketing system of time kind. If you want to really see what your numbers are and how you can work with them, you need to put 100% of your hours in the PSA (professional services automation tool). You can only get reports out if you put data in.

Lots of people have told me that they need to figure out how to make their technicians as "billable" as possible. Somehow in our heads, we think we can get a perfect technician to bill 40 hours a week. Unless the tech works 60 hours, you're not going to get 40 hours billable out of him!

Assuming a full time tech is working 40 hours/week . . . the best you can hope for is about 70% billable on a consistent basis. Technicians check email, sit in on company meetings, do training, watch webinars, etc. If you don't charge for travel both ways, then they spend time driving around unbillable.

I've heard people say their techs are 80% or 90% billable. But every time I hear that, I ask about how rigorous they are at tracking time. Does every technician account for every minute between 8:00 AM and 5:00 PM? The answer is invariably NO. So these folks have an impression that their technicians are super-billable, but they don't even know how much time they are logging on the job every week!

Copyright © 2014 Karl W. Palachuk

If you track this very carefully, you will discover that it is extremely uncommon for a tech to be more than 65% billable. Now, as we move to doing more and more work remotely, this number increases. As a tech's job moves from little jobs to big jobs, he becomes more billable.

Please see the following chapters:

- "Running Regular Financial Reports" – Volume One (This covers the ideas and expectations of billability).

- "Time Tracking for Employees" – Volume Three

- "Do Billable Work First?" – Volume Two

- "Working in Real Time" – Volume Three

What Does "Billable" Mean?

Let's begin by defining Billable Work. If you are in the world of break/fix, the definition is easy: *Billable work is labor for which you will invoice the client.* In this world, there are really only two kinds of work. There is work you give away for free and work you bill for. (Free labor includes rework or other work you intentionally do not charge for. There's a completely separate discussion about all the labor you give away for free because you don't properly track your time.)

In Managed Services, the discussion can be a little more complicated. "Project work" is just like break/fix above. You either bill for it or give it away. But with Managed Services, you have work that is covered by the service agreement. For example, all work to maintain the server might be covered. So checking the logs, applying fixes, and verifying that there's plenty of disc space is all covered work.

For our purposes, productive labor covered by a service agreement is considered billable. Rework and floundering around unproductively

Copyright © 2014 Karl W. Palachuk

trying to figure something out should be considered un-billable here as well, but it's very hard to track. The key point here is that "billable work" under a MSA (managed service agreement) includes work to fulfill the agreement. It is "time on task" and you will not invoice the client for it separately.

Billable Labor Hours per Week

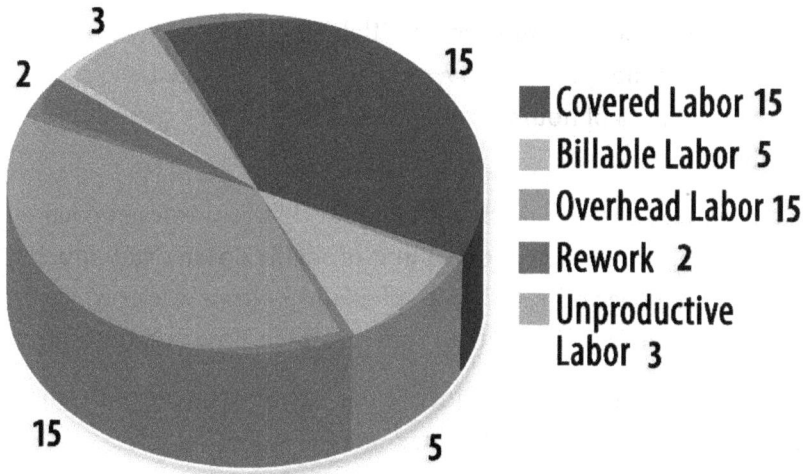

Covered Labor 15
Billable Labor 5
Overhead Labor 15
Rework 2
Unproductive Labor 3

See the pie chart. Of course your numbers will vary.

The chart represents an example of how time can be divided in a week. We start with 40 hours. Fifteen hours is "overhead" time. This represents meetings, training, driving, etc. as discussed above. This number will be larger for managers and smaller for dedicated technicians. Just remember that it can only get so small. So be realistic.

Another fifteen hours is work on covered machines. This includes whatever you have in your MSA. Two hours are rework. Another

Copyright © 2014 Karl W. Palachuk

three hours are otherwise unproductive. This unproductive work includes things like standing around waiting for another technician. Most commonly, it represents working on a problem and making no headway. This happens when you (your tech) bang your head against a problem for an hour or more and make no progress toward the solution.

Finally, we have five hours of truly billable labor. These are hours spend on Add-Move-Change tickets and billable project labor. For MSA clients, this is work not covered by the MSA.

When I say we want to **maximize billability**, I mean we want to increase the time spent on Covered Labor and Billable Labor. These are at about 50% of hours for the week. This is a very realistic number.

The Overhead time might be different for different roles in your company, as mentioned above. But it probably doesn't vary much for an individual over time. So if Joe spends 15 hours a week on Overhead, you cannot expect to squeeze much time out of this area.

That leaves two key areas for increasing billability: Reduce Rework and Reduce Unproductive Labor.

Reducing Rework and Reducing Unproductive Labor

So our culprits boil down to these two categories. You might be tempted to lump them both together under Unproductive Labor, but Rework really needs to be separate. Unproductive labor may not be related to competence. Rework means you (your tech) did something wrong and then they (or someone else) had to go do the work again. This is very often related to training, competence, and experience. You absolutely have to minimize rework.

Copyright © 2014 Karl W. Palachuk

Here are six things you can do to minimize these categories and increase billable hours.

1. Work from Highest Priority to Lowest Priority

This starts with assigning a priority to every single ticket or task. Everything in your company needs to be prioritized. Low priority tasks might be easy or even fun. But you have to be disciplined to work based on priority level. Search my blog for "priority" and you'll see lots of articles about why priorities are so important (http://blog.smallbizthoughts.com).

A lot of the low priority items fall into the category of *Urgent* but *Not Important*. Clearing up high priority tasks often clears up some smaller tasks that were related to the issue. It also guarantees that techs are working on the most important things. It is rare that high priority tasks are not covered under an MSA or truly billable.

2. Schedule Work, but Schedule it Loosely

The most productive work is planned. Time and time again I have to coach people that it's okay to tell a client that you schedule work two or three days out. Projects might be two or three weeks out. If you can plan to tackle specific jobs on specific days, you can organize the work and prepare for it. You can have the right tools and research.

Reactive work is always less effective. You jump off one task and onto another. That action automatically reduces the effectiveness of your work on the task you are abandoning. And because your work on the new problem is completely unplanned, you are less productive on that as well.

Copyright © 2014 Karl W. Palachuk

Here's what happens to the task you abandoned: When you go back to it, you have to figure out where you left off. It will take some time to come up to speed. Remember, you WERE up to speed on the problem when you abandoned it. The time spent coming back up to speed is not rework, but it is certainly unproductive labor – and unnecessary.

I say to schedule loosely because it gives you flexibility. Tell clients you'll be there on a specific day. If you need to, say morning or evening. As a general rule, that's much better than agreeing on a specific time. Specific time slots mean that you might have to stop doing one job to go do the scheduled job. See previous paragraph. It also means that you might have a time gap between jobs. Totally unproductive time.

In a perfect world, you won't rush from one emergency to another. You'll plan things out a day or two in advance. For each task, you'll complete it or come to a natural stopping point. Then you'll move on to the next task, minimizing the unproductive gap between jobs.

3. Develop and Encourage Specialization

For any given hardware or software, you will have a specific level of knowledge. Ideally, your team will include a variety of people with a variety of skills. If there are any products you consider critical to your success, you should have someone who specializes in the product. If this person is not on your team, then you should make sure you have access to them when you need them.

It is pretty obvious that someone with specialized knowledge will fix things faster. This reduces time spent floundering around trying to figure things out. Of course, once you solve a problem, you should take time to put notes in the ticket so you can replicate your success.

4. Call for Help

You should have a policy in your company that no one is allowed to work on a problem for very long without making progress. You might decide the limit is 15 minutes, 30 minutes, or even an hour. But at some point, they MUST call for help. They might call their manager, another technician, a friend at another company (if appropriate), the vendor's tech support line, or anyone else who can help.

In addition to a "fresh pair of eyes," calling for help immediately limits the amount of unproductive time that can accumulate in your company. You might even have lower limits for newer techs. Of course everyone should be using a Troubleshoot and Repair Log (TSR) to keep track of what they've done. See Chapter 30.

A TSR Log will allow other team members, or third party tech support, to come up to speed very quickly when you call for help. Many young techs refuse to call for help. Then they end up spending countless hours on something that another person might have fixed right away. Or perhaps the problem was known but undocumented, so no amount of research would reveal the fix. It takes a certain maturity and self-confidence to say that you don't see the answer and need help.

Interestingly enough, more experienced technicians tend to ask for "help" all the time. It is often the fastest path to success. We all have different experiences and perspectives.

5. Make Minimizing Rework a High Priority

There are many causes to rework. Making it a company-wide priority to minimize rework will have a dramatic effect. First, it makes

Copyright © 2014 Karl W. Palachuk

everyone aware of the need. So team members can enforce the goal of minimizing rework and help each other out. Second, it will make it easier for technicians to ask for help.

Third, making this a priority will lead to other actions that are good for your company overall. Without knowing anything about the specific rework, you can guarantee that it is related to either poor planning or lack of training/experience. So you need to make sure you have adequate training programs. These can be internal. In fact, sometimes internal training is the best because you can go at the student's pace, and you know the training is on YOUR way of doing something.

Planning is obviously good for any project. It is particularly good for avoiding rework. If you slow down and plan your work, you are much more likely to proceed from start to finish without retracing your steps.

6. Documentation is Your Friend

You knew I had to throw this in the mix. Documentation includes procedures and planning. It includes TSR Logs. It includes putting all of your notes and hours in the PSA. It includes using checklists – and only checking each box after the task is complete.

When you know exactly what you have done and not done, troubleshooting becomes a lot easier. Ideally, you should be able to read through the notes on a ticket and come up to speed very quickly on the problem and what has been tried so far.

If the client has a similar problem in the future, you'll have the answer at your fingertips. If other clients have a similar problem, you'll still have the answer at your fingertips.

Copyright © 2014 Karl W. Palachuk

Final Thoughts

What do we do for a living? We implement, maintain, and troubleshoot. Implementation can be very efficient with proper planning. But it's not perfect. Maintenance should be very easy, but it's not perfect. And troubleshooting is certainly not a perfect science.

So it is impossible to totally eliminate rework or unproductive labor. You can minimize it. But you can't eliminate it.

Maximizing billability, therefore, is also not a science. It takes constant attention and effort. It takes proper training and a company-wide ethic of reducing unproductive labor. (Note that training is time spent in the "overhead labor" category.) This is not something you can implement and walk away from. Maximizing billability is a never-ending job.

It relies on excellent time tracking, excellent documentation, excellent planning, excellent training, and excellent teamwork to support each other to eliminate rework and unproductive labor.

Copyright © 2014 Karl W. Palachuk

3 and 3

Three Take-Aways from This Chapter:

1. In order to calculate true billability, you need to define what is truly billable – and then track it rigorously.

2. You may perceive that your team is highly billable when they are not.

3. Rework is the worst kind of un-billable labor. It is generally eliminated by training and experience.

Three Action Steps for Your Company:

1. _____

   _____

2. _____

   _____

3. _____

   _____

Copyright © 2014 Karl W. Palachuk

20

Email Rules and Etiquette for the Consultant

Email has been the "killer app" since networking began – way before the Internet. It still is THE killer app. But email can also be a massive time-wasting distraction. How the technician manages email can affect service delivery and profitability. Plus it can have a dramatic effect on customer relationships.

For the consultant, we're primarily interested in Email processes and procedures that help you manage time effectively. Once you agree on a process for this, you need to write it up, train your people, and hold each other accountable.

You do not need to follow the process exactly, but you should work on the assumption that everyone in the company follows the same general pattern for their day. At the end I discuss how and why you should avoid the email time-suck. This really does apply to you. Yes you.

Do Not Be Interrupt-Driven

This applies to many elements of your personal and work life. It is particularly true with email. Go into the Outlook settings and turn off all notifications. No dings, no changing icons, no flashing screens. And absolutely no little pop-up in the corner that takes your attention away from what you're doing.

Everyone in your company should have ALL of these interruptions turned off. Period. They add nothing to your productivity and serve no purpose except to keep you addicted to switching tasks and reducing your attention span.

A few people need their email open all the time. But most technicians do not need it open all day. They need it open while checking email. Other than that, it should be closed.

Checking Email

You should process your email a minimum of three times per day. Start with Morning, Noon, and late in the work day. Set specific times if it's helpful. For example, on odd-numbered hours (9am, 11am, 1pm, 3pm).

Everyone needs to check their email and appropriately act on the content in a timely manner. This is especially true of inter-office emails. Quite often we need answers from our fellow techs to be able to proceed, and a quick response means the least time lost in momentum for the work at hand.

DO NOT camp out on your inbox and DO NOT attend to any email that pops up.

Unless you are waiting on an email for the project, activity, or Service Request that you are currently working on, only process email when you are between tasks and have set aside time to do it.

Anything else is interrupt driven and only causes you to waste time. Changing tasks distracts your focus.

Processing Email

Everyone at your company should follow the same email retention practices. Here's what we recommend.

First, create a year folder in Outlook Public Folders. For example, 2014 for the current year. Inside that you will create sub-folders related to everything that is important company-wide.

Subfolders might include

- Clients

- Marketing

- Operations

- Products and Services

Within Clients, create a subfolder for each client. I don't recommend that you save every single email from every client. But whenever something is important, such as a discussion about a hardware sale, then file it in the client public folder.

This is an easy way to make sure everyone has access to all the information in your email system that's relevant to specific clients, vendors, etc. Other than matters of a personal or financial nature, all important communications should be in the public folders.

It should NEVER be the case that an important client communication is in the mailbox of one technician and not visible to others.

Even as a sole proprietor, this is a great habit to get into.

Note: At the end of the year you can create the 2015 folder and have a nice little archive of 2014 information. You could even save last year to a PST file and keep it on the server. You could open a local copy if needed.

Second, deal with email in batches.

Early in the day, when you're settling in, is the time to look at the latest Microsoft Partner Newsletter or the latest blast from some vendor. Once you open it, though, DEAL with it. That means read it, file it, forward it, or delete it. If you delete the same newsletter regularly without reading it, unsubscribe.

The rest of the day, do not look at any email unless it is related to business. That means, internal emails, or emails related to your current projects, service requests, or activities.

This process is very simple and allows anyone to clear their mail box quickly, efficiently, and not end up with 75 unread messages containing client requests for help or information aging away.

How To Read and Process An Email Message

For each and every email in the inbox, do only one of the following actions:

- Reply to it and then Delete or Move the email to another folder

- Act on it immediately and then Delete or Move the email to another folder

- Forward it and then Delete or Move the email to another folder

- Create a service request and then Delete or Move the email to another folder

- Create an Activity in your PSA system and then Delete or Move the email to another folder

- Just delete it

Rinse, Repeat.

Note on business related emails:

Always enter time or notes to any related SR immediately! If you do not do it now it will get lost.

Logging Your Time

It takes time to process email. We process time in 15 minute increments. It is highly unlikely that you will open an email and proceed to bill time to a client (or log time against a managed service agreement). See Chapter Seventeen.

If you do log eight or more minutes dealing with a client issue, then you should log fifteen minutes to the appropriate service agreement. But more commonly, you will log your time as internal and administrative.

This is very handy for determining how much time employees are wasting "getting going" in the morning. If someone logs two hours to checking email in one day, they probably need to find a new profession. Just sayin.

But you don't know how much time is spent on email unless you track it.

Copyright © 2014 Karl W. Palachuk

Avoid the Email Time-Suck

You already know this: Email is the greatest officially approved time waster in your business. If you have no rules around it, then it be like a wild vine. It will find its own path and fill up empty space without being noticed.

Email makes us extremely productive and is a great tool for managing information. At the same time, email can waste resources such as time and disc space. It can distract you from more important jobs. And it can interrupt you when you need to focus.

Some companies simply do not allow individual technicians to have email. That seems difficult, but the advantages are obvious.

You don't have to follow these guidelines exactly. But you should have some policy to limit how much email distracts you and your employees. To the extent that it's a productive tool, use it. To the extent that it's a distracting time-suck, limit it.

Implementing this policy follows the common process. First, you need to write up your email rules. Second, you need to train your employees on the procedure. Third, you need to support each other and remind each other of the policy.

3 and 3

Three Take-Aways from This Chapter:

1. It should NEVER be the case that an important client communication is in the mailbox of one technician and not visible to others.

2. The norm across your entire organization should be to avoid being interrupt-driven.

3. If you feel resistance to the advice here, it is probably fear. Examine that fear and address it. Then follow this advice.

Three Action Steps for Your Company:

1. _____

   _____

2. _____

   _____

3. _____

   _____

Copyright © 2014 Karl W. Palachuk

Copyright © 2014 Karl W. Palachuk

21

Technician Supplies -- The "Scary Box"

No matter how small your business is, you will need to provide your techs with certain supplies. The nature of what you need to provide changes over time. But you should have an official list and make sure your techs have what they need. A $4 cable becomes a $60 cable if you have to pay your technician to drive back to the office and pick it up!

We provide technicians with a plastic Rubbermaid-type box to carry in their trunk. It keeps the materials safe and orderly. In addition, this makes it easy for the tech to take these materials out of the trunk as needed. We call this the "Scary box" because it gets disorderly pretty fast. When techs are stressed out or in a hurry, they tend to dig through the box and never get around to straightening it out.

We have techs bring the box to their quarterly review. It is never in order. Really. But the quarterly review is a time to get it back in order and make sure all supplies are up to spec.

What Every Technician Should Carry

So what's in the "Scary Box?"

Basically, there are three types of things the tech needs to carry: Tools, Office Supplies, and Parts. The list I give here is actually more than we normally carry these days. We've found that we carry fewer and fewer parts as time goes by. The reason for this is simple: Almost

Copyright © 2014 Karl W. Palachuk

nothing breaks any more. When was the last time you replaced a bad network card?

Tools

(Quantity = 1 each)

- Ground Strap
- Label Machine – with good batteries
- Network crossover cable or block
- Spare label tape
- 5 port network switch
- Philips screw (small)
- Philips screw (standard)
- Flat screw driver (small)
- Flat screw driver (standard)

Note: A tech may need other specific tools for a job. These should be provided, but don't need to live in the scary box for each technician.

Office Supplies

(Quantities vary, but you should have at least 3-5 of each item.)

- Manila pouch folders
- Tabs for Network Documentation Binders
- The Company Product labels (If you put a company sticker with the date on every piece of hardware you install.)
- Labels for Offsite Backups

Copyright © 2014 Karl W. Palachuk

- "I was at your computer" memos
- Equipment Disposal Verification Forms
- CD Sleeves

Parts

- DAT 160 Cleaning Cartridges
- DAT 160 Tapes
- Network Controller Card
- 50' Network cable Qty 1
- 25' Network cable Qty 1
- 10' Network cable Qty 3
- 7' Network cable Qty 3
- 5' Network cable Qty 5
- 3' Network cable Qty 5
- SATA control cable
- Velcro ties
- USB Cable - Standard A to B
- USB Cable - Type A to Mini
- USB Cable - Type A to Micro

Unlike some businesses (e.g., cabling companies), we need to be very careful to keep the inventory piece of this very small. As technology changes, you are very likely to have some leftover cables or other

Copyright © 2014 Karl W. Palachuk

items that you never use. I think we have five or six old style parallel printer cables at our office.

Even though each of these is not very expensive, as a whole they represent a significant chunk of change. In fact, as we phase out tape backups, we have eliminated tapes from the scary box. At $100-$200 per box, this is not a minor investment. You need to balance the need for these items with the cost.

A Few Notes About Taking Care of Supplies

The technician is expected to maintain a supply of the items listed (from The Company stock) at all times. If something is used up or sold out of the tech's supply, they need to get it restocked as soon as possible. The intention is to never be on site without something you should always have on hand.

Once the list of items is assembled and inventoried, the technician is to sign for the list of supplies. (You should have a form for signing out keys, security cards, and other company property.) A copy of their list will be maintained in their employee file. Once created, only major item additions and deletions will be tracked. The technician is ultimately responsible for the care and inventory of the items.

Any delivery to a client, loss, damage, theft or other disposition of an item is expected to be reported to The Company in the appropriate manner as soon as possible. That is to say, if an item is delivered or left for a client to own and use it must be entered on the product tab of some SR in a timely manner so that it can get correctly billed. If an item is dropped, otherwise damaged, etc. it must be brought to the service manager's attention immediately. The preferred method of informing the service manager is via email.

Copyright © 2014 Karl W. Palachuk

It is reasonably expected that the technician will safeguard any The Company property appropriately. It is expected that it will never be left in an unlocked vehicle or left in any vehicle overnight in a location that could be considered a high crime district.

Copyright © 2014 Karl W. Palachuk

3 and 3

Three Take-Aways from This Chapter:

1. While keeping your inventory to a minimum, you should provide techs with some of the items they are most likely to need while out in the field.

2. If you find that you consistently need something, add it to your Scary Box supply list. If you stop needing something, take it off.

3. Don't skip the quarterly checks. No matter what you do, most techs will not be diligent about keeping supplies in order.

Three Action Steps for Your Company:

1. _____

_____

2. _____

_____

3. _____

_____

Copyright © 2014 Karl W. Palachuk

22

Final Friday Training

Once you begin to have employees, there are several things you need to add to your "To Do" list. One is constant training. New technology comes out all the time. Technicians need to improve continually. A second thing you add to your routine is the creation of culture.

Company culture is the perfect example of why planning and goal-setting are important. If you don't "create" a culture, it will create itself. You don't have to have some big master scheme. But you should have some intentions about what you want. The more you try to create a culture, the more successful you'll be.

Final Friday Training is a great way to address both of these needs. You might do something for Tuesday Lunch or Thursday Breakfast. We do Final Friday Training as a way to build the team and keep them trained at the same time. Here's how it works:

1. We pick a topic for technical training

2. We all gather for lunch in the office

3. Most of lunchtime is just talking and enjoying ourselves

4. After lunch we spend 1-2 hours on the training. Normally it is conducted by the most technical staff member. But sometimes it's run by a lower level tech with specialized knowledge. This includes training on a new PSA system, a new backup system, a new operating system, etc.

Copyright © 2014 Karl W. Palachuk

5. After the training we normally break up and disperse slowly. Because we hold our training on Friday afternoon, someone needs to check the service board. A few tickets may need to be finished up before the weekend.

But overall, the day ends very leisurely and low stress. You may even choose to let some folks leave early.

Don't be unclear about this point: This is a technical training. You need to really use this time to improve the technical abilities of your team. Help them improve themselves. Continually improve. Always moving up.

The team building piece will happen naturally. You're just using the technical training to give them an opportunity to get to know each other better.

Practical Considerations

Here's how we actually execute our Final Friday:

- There is an auto generated Service Request that will show up the third week of every month. This gives plenty of time for everyone to see it on their schedule and be ready for it.

- All technicians are assigned to the service request and scheduled for the last half of the day from 1pm to 5 pm.

- There is a document in the shared storage area (SharePoint, cloud drive, mapped drive, etc.) called "Final Friday Training Topics.docx" that lists all suggested and completed subjects for the Final Friday training.

- All technicians are expected to attend and encouraged to take a turn in presenting training.

Copyright © 2014 Karl W. Palachuk

Final Friday Training Topics

Obviously you will create your own list, adding training specific to your company and your offerings. Here are some of the topics we've covered over the years:

- DNS/IP/DHCP/etc
- Intelligent Disaster Recovery
- Exchange / Active Dir Tools
- PIX configuration and setting
- SMTP TSR and the Deep Six
- Troubleshooting SMTP
- IIS settings on SBS including SMTP, DNS and DHCP changes
- RDP and Shadowing session
- Veritas Accounts
- Anti-Virus setup and maintenance
- RMM Monitoring
- Outlook profiles (Exch & Pop)
- Hosted Spam Filter
- Patch Scripting
- FireFox FireWall
- Office "preferred" settings
- Windows Desktop preferred settings
- Clean corrupt files out of older Exchange files so Back Up exec does not report "Bad items"
- Thin Client lockdown

- Veritas Configuration

- The power of a reboot

- Example SR's for how we do repeat work:

    o Use actual (resolved) service requests as examples of solving specific problems

- Handy things to know and master

    o RDP to console

    o RDP session sharing

    o Client data folders

    o RMM logs on local machine

    o Setting up RMM agents

Implementation

We started this practice when there were just three of us. It's easy to set the calendar, but it can be hard to get out of the trenches and actually do what you know is in your company's best interest.

This is a higher-level activity and should be treated as such. That means it is more important than low-level tasks and tickets; more important than medium tasks and ticket. If you have true emergencies, of course they need to be handled. But don't start making excuses.

I know this four hours can seem unproductive when there's a backlog of work. But you're only doing this twelve times a year. And whether you choose First Friday or Final Friday, there's bound to be a holiday or two that interfere. Be flexible, but not too flexible. Build that habit!

Copyright © 2014 Karl W. Palachuk

3 and 3

Three Take-Aways from This Chapter:

1. Regular training – on any schedule that works for you – keeps your technicians sharp and builds your team.

2. You only do this 10-12 times per year. Take it seriously. Make it a priority.

3. When you assign a technician to learn something new, ask them to turn around and teach it to the rest of the team.

Three Action Steps for Your Company:

1. _____

_____

2. _____

_____

3. _____

_____

Copyright © 2014 Karl W. Palachuk

Copyright © 2014 Karl W. Palachuk

Section III

Client Management

Copyright © 2014 Karl W. Palachuk

Copyright © 2014 Karl W. Palachuk

23

Setup a New Managed Service Client (Checklist)

This chapter covers a topic that I hope you get to use a lot. It covers a key piece of "on-boarding" a new managed service client. I go into this in much more detail in the book *Managed Services in a Month*. But here's the key checklist part.

This checklist assumes that someone has already made the deal and achieved a signed contract. Now you need to move them into your "system" as full clients. That means they need to get into your billing system, your ticketing system, your monitoring system, etc.

I'll present the basic checklist first and then make some comments. This process assumes that you have several functions in place. If you don't, you should. If your shop is small, then you may play all the roles. But you need to build the company you wish to become.

When we were moving lots of clients over to the new contracts, we used this list a lot. All of these lists need to have a work flow that makes sense. Some work is done by the tech department, some by admin, etc. And someone has to keep track of these documents so they don't get stalled somewhere along the way. Ideally, everything on this list will be achieved in 1-2 days.

A Word .docx version of this checklist is included in the downloads associated with this book.

The Checklist for Setting Up a New Managed Service Client

Outline – New Managed Services Client Checklist

New Client / Signer: _____

Date: _____

Signed Deal (circle one)   Silver   -   Gold   -   Platinum

First Month on Service will be: _____

Cover Sheet

of Servers: _____

Cost for Servers: _____

# of Workstations: _____

Cost for Workstations: _____

Monthly total: _____

Setup Fees: _____

Setup to be paid by (circle one)   Check   Credit Card

Monthly to be paid by (choose one)

- Check (3 months)
- Credit Card each month

Correct Billing Information:

Company: _____

Name: _____

Address 1: _____

Address 2: _____

City / State / Zip: _____ _____ _____

Contact Phone: _____

For each of the following items, note the Person Responsible and the Date Completed.

Administration:

- Create Service Request (enter time estimate 1.5 hrs)

    o At this point, the Service Request will be worked by the Admin department until handed over to Tech Support.

- Check to see that the names match how they want to be billed for services:

    o in PSA

    o in QuickBooks

    o on the Company Mailing List

    o Create Invoices for Setup / monthly (See amounts above)

    o Calculate first month fees + setup Sales

    o Collect Money:

- If Credit Card:

    o Collect Credit Card form

    o Charge Credit card: initial setup fees/first month

    o Apply payments in QB

    o Set up Autopay & Monthly recurring

    o Remove old recurring charges from credit card

Copyright © 2014 Karl W. Palachuk

- If Check:

    o   Collect check from client (3 months + setup)

    o   Apply payments in QB

    o   Put check with other checks to be deposited

- File all paperwork

- Create credits as needed for services that had been sold individually (spam filtering, monitoring, other)

- Expire old service agreements in Autotask/ConnectWise

- Create service agreements in Autotask/ConnectWise

- Create reports as needed in Continuum/Level Platforms (or whatever you use)

- Change SR to "Schedule This"

Tech Dept:

At this point, the Service Request will be worked by the Tech Support department until it's time for client training.

- Update Managed Services Grid

- Set up Monitoring, Schedule Patches, Fixes

- Set up hosted spam filter, if appropriate

- Set up hosted Exchange, if appropriate

- Set up hosted storage, if appropriate

- Train Client on hosted spam filter

- Install RMM agent on client PCs (create a separate SR)

- Install RMM agent on servers (create a separate SR)

Copyright © 2014 Karl W. Palachuk

- Add server to daily monitoring (or verify)

- Add server to patch management group (or verify)

- Set up back up job alerts (or verify)

- Update daily monitoring sheet to include new client requirements

- Create the Monthly Maintenance Checklist for client

- Create the monthly single for client

- Check existing clients for compliance with the monthly maintenance and monthly single process

Training:

Your client training might be provided by techs, Customer Service Reps, Sales Dept., or someone else.

- Tutor client contact re: PSA portal

- Tutor client contact re: Our company Service Request process, priorities, and response times

- Send intro letter to client

Last Action:

- When all complete, put this form in to filing in-box

So there's the form and the flow. Sales to Admin to Tech to training.

Just like on-boarding an employee, you need a checklist for on-boarding a client. After a month or so, you'll assume all these things are done. But if you get into a discussion about what a "Priority One"

Copyright © 2014 Karl W. Palachuk

is, you'll feel a lot more comfortable if you can point back to the training you did.

And you know you did it because it's on the checklist!

Of course your process will be a little different. Change as needed. Above all else, you need a consistent process that can give you repeated success.

Copyright © 2014 Karl W. Palachuk

3 and 3

Three Take-Aways from This Chapter:

1. A smooth client on-boarding process goes a long ways to improving the client's impression of your company.

2. Create a client on-boarding checklist and guarantee you don't forget some little thing with each client.

3. Use the client on-boarding checklist to train your staff to see the big picture of customer relations.

Three Action Steps for Your Company:

1. _____

   _____

2. _____

   _____

3. _____

   _____

Copyright © 2014 Karl W. Palachuk

Copyright © 2014 Karl W. Palachuk

24

Client Personnel Changes - New User Checklist

You have a process for bringing a new employee onboard (well, you should anyway). So what about when *your clients* hire new employees? They will be added to the network and to managed services. As with everything else, your life will be easier if you have a standard process for this.

Before the Hire

This is a bit of a minor point, but it's one of those little things that can be very irritating: The client should give you as much advance notice as possible before they hire a new employee. The worst case scenario is when you get a call at 8:01 AM on a Monday to tell you that the new hire is showing up at 9:00 AM for training. Can you please set up a new workstation for her?

Oh wait. The worst case scenario is that she needs a new PC as well.

In most cases, the hiring process will include defining the job, advertising the job, gathering resumes, weeding through resumes, one or two interviews, and a job offer. There are few "emergency" job hires. So clients need to engage you well before the new hire shows up. Luckily, managed services makes this easy. See the New Hire

Copyright © 2014 Karl W. Palachuk

Flowchart. Basically, they can create a service ticket at any time. It can sit there for weeks if needed, as long as the due date is set correctly.

Adding a New User to Client's Managed Services

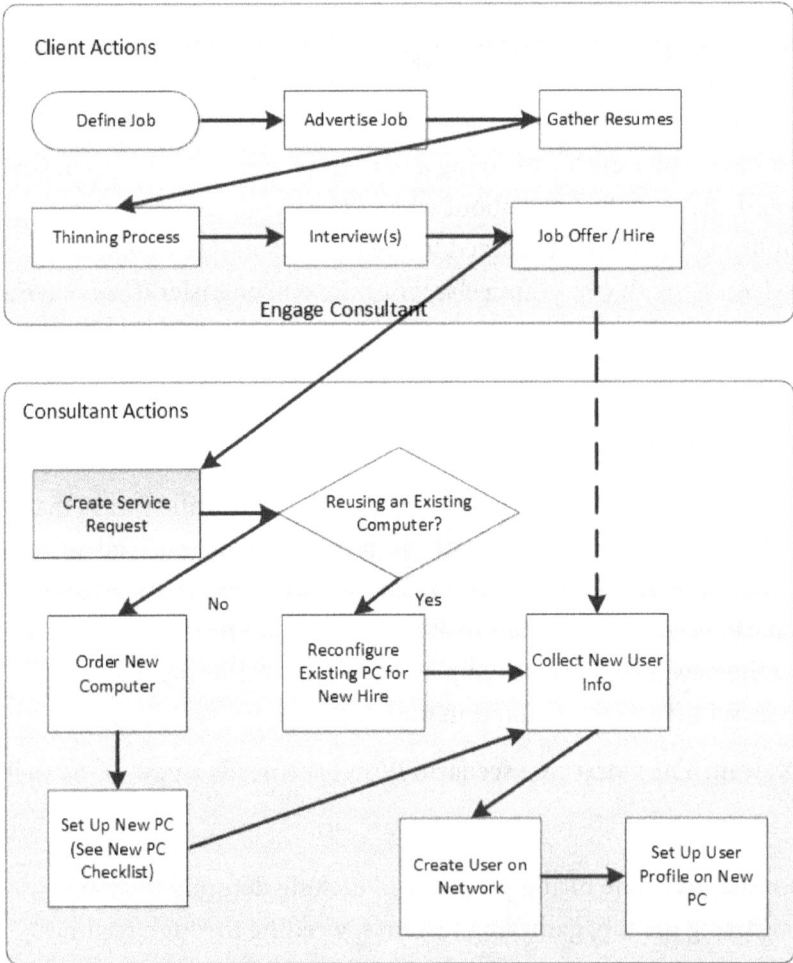

New User Checklist

The actual New User Checklist has three sections. As you can see, there's a lot less if you have the User's name before you start. But you need to adjust as needed. In many cases, you need to set up the PC in advance and add the user at the last minute.

A Word .docx version of this check list is included with the downloadable material associated with this book.

 The three sections are:

1) Client / User Information

2) Set up the Computer (hardware and software)

3) User-Specific Setups

Section One: Client / User Information

Technician (work performed by) : _____

Date: _____

Client Info: _____

• Company: _____

• Address: _____

• Contact: _____

• Phone: _____

New User Name: _____

New User's Logon: _____

and Password: _____

New User's Machine / Workstation Name: _____

Local Administrator password: _____

Section Two: Set up the Computer

(Note: This section will be replaced by your "New PC Checklist." (See Volume Four in this series.) I'm just giving an abbreviated example here.

1. Set time and Region within Windows

2. If machine is not part of the domain, add machine to domain

3. Log on as domain administrator and add domain users to local administrators group

4. Map drives required by this user (if not handles by logon script). Install cloud drive if needed.

5. If things need to be copied locally, create C:\!Tech directory

6. Install Adobe Acrobat Reader latest version

7. Install printers to be used by this user

8. Install Anti-Virus and updates. Schedule scans.

9. Install Microsoft Office products

10. Apply all Windows Updates

Copyright © 2014 Karl W. Palachuk

Section Three: User-Specific Setups

(Perform these tasks while logged on as the new user)

1. Set up Outlook to point to client's Exchange Server

2. Connect user to shared calendars and resources within Outlook

3. Set up Company Contacts as an Outlook address book

4. Verify that drives are mapped (this is controlled by logon script, not locally)

5. Set up Line of Business application shortcut and all other shortcuts normally required by this client

6. Verify that you can browse the Internet

7. Verify that you can send and receive email from an outside address (preferably a domain on a different Internet Service Provider and on a different hosted spam filter).

8. Verify that you can access company data drive(s)

9. Verify that you can print to each printer

The Human Connection

We love our clients. They love us. That starts on Day One when they learn to use our system properly. When they learn to use our system properly, they get the fastest tech support. When they call and call and never create a service ticket, they get a slower response. Because we want their love, we need to train them to use our service efficiently.

So – you guessed it – training the new employee about our system is just as important as showing them how to log on to their computer. We give them a link to our Client Service Portal. We walk them

Copyright © 2014 Karl W. Palachuk

through entering a service request. And we give them a human connection along with their new job and their new computer.

Implementation

Implementing this process is pretty easy. It assumes you have a New PC Checklist for each client. THIS process will also be customized for each client. You may even enter IP addresses for printers and other devices that don't change often.

Unlike most processes, the first part of this one requires you to engage your client and ask them to give you notice as soon as possible. You can show them your flowchart, like the one above. Describe enough of the process that they get the message that planning makes everything easier. (Don't describe so much detail that they fall asleep and smack their head on the desk.)

You might create a folder on your company's shared drive of SharePoint site to hold all the client New User Checklists along with the New PC Checklists. You really should customize these for each client.

Don't forget documentation. That means that the info from Section One and all other relevant information go into your PSA system and into the client's on-site documentation.

After every new user setup, the last item on the checklist should be to update the checklist! That way, it is always as useful as possible. When you added that new network scanner, you should have documented it – but you probably didn't update the New PC Checklist or New User Checklist. This will be apparent when you go through the checklist, so just make sure it's updated for next time.

Copyright © 2014 Karl W. Palachuk

This kind of policy requires that everyone on the team

1) Be aware of the policy

2) Practice the policy

3) Correct one another's errors

4) Support one another with reminders

Copyright © 2014 Karl W. Palachuk

3 and 3

Three Take-Aways from This Chapter:

1. Help the client to engage you as early as possible in the process of setting up a new user.

2. Start with the basic New User checklist here, but eventually create a New PC Checklist for each client.

3. Training the clients early on is a great way to help them to use your system – and make the entire relationship better over time.

Three Action Steps for Your Company:

1. _____

   _____

2. _____

   _____

3. _____

   _____

Copyright © 2014 Karl W. Palachuk

25

Client Personnel Changes - Employee Departure Checklist

In the last chapter, we talked about what to do when a client hires a new employee. This chapter will address the other side of that issue: When a client's employee leaves.

Obviously, employees leave for lots of reasons. They take new jobs, get married, move for family reasons, get fired, get promoted to another office, etc. So departures need to be handled differently. In addition, companies have different security needs and SOPs (standard operating procedures) that affect employee departures.

As with so many changes, we have to be careful about how we remove users from the network. While it is unlikely that a user will return, it's certainly possible. At a minimum, their data need to be protected. That means their Outlook data, locally stored files, personalized database data, and so forth. Even after the user's logon has been disabled and deleted, some of their data will remain and you need to be able to find it.

Reading through this procedure, you'll notice that the keyword here is "deliberate." That means you're going to go slow, be careful, and don't make anything irreversible until it needs to be.

Copyright © 2014 Karl W. Palachuk

Procedure for Users Exit from a Company

Step One. Request to Disable or Delete a User From The Network

When a Client has an employee or contractor leave the company, there is a standard list of steps to be taken. The nature of the user exit must be determined in case there are additional actions to be taken. If there are security concerns, a more immediate response is required in disabling the account.

Of course all actions must be within a service request. So you must create a service request in your PSA as soon as you receive a request from the client.

Note: A Word .docx version of this checklist is included with the downloadable material for this book.

- Communicate with the client contact to determine the best action based on their situation and needs

- Create a service request with the contact as your primary company contact – not the person who is leaving the company

- If there is any reason to believe the employee or contractor exit is hasty and un-amicable take all necessary action to protect the client and their system first

- Determine Nature of user Exit

- If necessary, disable the users account right away and change the password

- Compose and send an email to the client contact using the template "Request to disable or delete a user from the network - Initial Request" from the email templates directory. Make sure a copy of this gets into the service request.

Copyright © 2014 Karl W. Palachuk

Step Two: Disabling or Deleting a User From The Network

Note: After the user is deleted from the network, do not run the Exchange mailbox cleanup agent until a full backup has gone off site for the month.

Once you have received the reply with all the required information, proceed as follows:

- Change the departing user's domain account password. In general, it's a good practice to change the password or disable the account and leave it that way for 30 days. The final step will be to wait 30 days and then delete the account.

- If necessary, change passwords for other existing accounts that user may have access to. This includes financial programs, databases, line of business applications, etc.

- Document the password changes

- Reassign the user's SMTP addresses in Exchange as outlined in the client contacts email

- Reassign the user's SMTP addresses in the email spam filter as outlined in the client contacts email

- Delete the user's Email spam filter account

- Log onto the user's workstation as the departing user

- Export all of the user's email to a single archive file named "User_Name's archived email YYYYMMDD.pst".

  o Note: Do not choose to encrypt the file or use a password. You'll be storing it on a secure network drive.

- Move (not copy) the .pst file to the clients "\Archived Email" directory

- Assign user access to the.pst as outlined in the client contacts email (Default is to assign Everyone)

- Move (not copy) the users data from My Documents, Desktop and anywhere else it may be located on the workstation to the server "\Archived Users Data\'s archived data" directory

- Move (not copy) the users data from their Users personal folder on the network to the server "\Archived Users Data\'s archived data" directory. Do not move My Music, My Pictures or My Videos unless explicitly requested by the client.

- The directory structure would look like this

    o Company Data\ Archived Users Data\Tom's archived data\My Documents

    o Company Data\ Archived Users Data\Tom's archived data\Desktop

    o Company Data\ Archived Users Data\Tom's archived data\Users folder

- Assign user access to these directories and files as outlined in the client contacts email (Default is to assign Everyone)

- Removed the user contact from the PSA system

- Compose and send an email to the client contact using the template "Request to disable or delete a user from the network - Request Completed" from the email templates directory

- Change the service request status to "Schedule" and schedule it for 30 days in the future. The final action in the service request should be:

    o Remove the user from the domain and be certain the checkbox is checked to "Remove user's home folder"

Copyright © 2014 Karl W. Palachuk

Implementation Notes

The first thing you need to do is to create your version of this checklist. In many cases, you'll want to personalize this for every client. Just as with New PC checklists (see Volume Four), and many other tasks, having client-specific checklists (and folders) will make you much more efficient.

After you create your checklist, you need to write up your version of this process. You might not use email and a ticketing system as we do. So make sure the process flow works for you.

Finally, you'll need to train your technicians and then remind them that you have this process when it's needed. Clients don't lose people very often, so you might not use this procedure very often. It's important to remember you have it! Not only that, but you will need to be extremely careful in your documentation because no one in your company will get a chance to use this all the time. That means it needs to be written well enough for a first-timer to follow.

The templates mentioned in this procedure are below.

Email Template: Request to disable or delete a user from the network

Hello ,

This email is to request information regarding the Service Request to disable or delete a user from the network. This information is required to proceed.

Our normal procedure is as follows:

1. Disable the user account so no one can log in as that user

Copyright © 2014 Karl W. Palachuk

2. Redirect their internet email to someone else in the company if need be

3. Export all of their email to a single archive file in a public directory on the server

4. Move all the company data the user may have had on their workstation to public directories on the server

5. Delete the user from the network

We need the following to proceed:

1. What is the user's full name?

2. What is the name of the computer they have been using?

3. If the user's internet email is still to be accepted, to which user should we point it?

4. When we export all of their current and old email to a single archive file, who will need access to it? Note: Typically we do not restrict access to the archive file.

5. Where should we move any company data we find in the user's personal folders or on their workstation? Note: Typically we put it into the most public file area on the server so it can be sorted and assimilated.

6. Is there any reason this user should not be completely deleted from the system?

Thank you.

Copyright © 2014 Karl W. Palachuk

Template: Request to disable or delete a user from the network - Completed

Hello ,

We have completed your Service Request to disable or delete a user from the network.

The user has been deleted.

The user's internet email has been redirected to _____.

The users email has been exported to a single archive file called 's archived email *YYYYMMDD*.pst in the \Archived Email directory.

The following users have access to the file: *Everyone.*

Remember, only one user can have the file open at any given time.

The user's data has been moved from their personal folder on the server and their workstation to the \Archived Users Data\'s archived data directory.

The following users have access to these files: *Everyone.*

If there is anything else we can do for you please give us a call.

Thank you.

Copyright © 2014 Karl W. Palachuk

3 and 3

Three Take-Aways from This Chapter:

1. As you can see, there's lots of details involved in properly cleaning up after an employee departs. Make sure you client knows this!

2. With luck, you won't use this very much, so make sure the document is well written.

3. You should prepare these "departure" procedures for each client before they are needed. Being able to go through this process in short order is awesome customer service. Makes you look good, too..

Three Action Steps for Your Company:

1. _____

   _____

2. _____

   _____

3. _____

   _____

Copyright © 2014 Karl W. Palachuk

26

Activating and Registering Client Software and Hardware

One of the most annoying things you'll ever come across is a new client who doesn't "own" the software on their systems. Their hardware is not registered to them. They have no warranties. The services that must be registered are not in the names or emails of anyone in the company.

In most cases, this client has no documentation.

So the former consultant disappears one day, or gets fired. You come in and look around. You can't log into the firewall or the server. Eventually you have to replace the firewall, crack into the server, sell the client a bunch of legal software and new hardware. You get the idea.

In end, you have to charge the client thousands of dollars for the goods and services they supposedly already bought from someone else. It's a horrible, despicable situation.

This kind of behavior makes me ashamed to be in the same business as these consultants. They are thieves and low life scum. But we see this again and again.

One of the reasons I developed the documentation that eventually became *The Network Documentation Workbook* is to guarantee to my clients that I would never leave them in such a situation. As I say in

Copyright © 2014 Karl W. Palachuk

that book, the client owns the software, the hardware, the network, and the documentation. It is dishonorable and dishonest to leave them in the situation described above.

Your policies around software and hardware should focus on more than the basic rule that you should act honorably. Your policies should be clear, honest, and provide a sustainable process that contributes to the smooth operation and future profitability of your client.

Here are some basic policies we use to manage software and hardware with our clients.

Software Policies

Installation

When we sell software to a client, we always install that software. Unless there are extreme circumstances, we install the software and we charge the client for doing so. Our managed service agreement states that all software must be installed by us. In addition, it states

that all labor necessary to fix machines after someone else (including the client) installs software is billable.

It may not seem to you or your client that software installation is a skill worthy of a $125/hr technician. But it is. If you don't believe me, watch three or four of your clients install software. They put things in strange places. They don't choose the right options. They do it differently every time.

This is what you do for a living, and you will be careful to make sure that you can support the software you install. If the client does it, you don't know what actions they took or decisions they made. That can make it more expensive for you to support.

Activation

We always activate software. Whatever the process, we make sure that this is taken care of. Some clients react favorably to a popup that asks them to activate software. Others will call on the phone or even log off their computer. It is a simple thing to activate the software and make it a non-issue.

This also eliminates the question of whether the installation is complete, so you can check the last box on the installation checklist!

Registration

We generally do not register software unless it is required for support services. Normally, registration benefits the manufacturer and not the purchaser. It results in spam but few benefits, if any.

Of course, if product activation requires it, then we do register the software.

Licensing

All licenses must be legally registered/recorded in the client's name. They paid for it. It's theirs.

Copyright © 2014 Karl W. Palachuk

- Custom Installation

We always choose "custom" installation when given the option. There are two primary reasons for this. First, if the software includes default options to install tool bars and demo software, we don't want that. Second, the default options may not always be the best choice. For example, many options are disabled by default in Microsoft Office.

Hardware Policies

Registration

As with software, all hardware that needs to be registered should be registered in the client's name. The same arguments apply.

Lifespan

It is our core belief that a business class machine's useful life is three years. Even if it is in perfectly working condition after three years, it's truly "useful" life is over. It is slow by today's standards. The hard drive is too small. It doesn't have enough memory. It doesn't have the latest ports and hardware options.

Upgrading Hardware

We do not upgrade hardware in machines that are more than 3 years old. It has been our repeated experience that either there will be a significant loss of time vs. profit just getting the correct parts from our supplier, or some other hardware issue will exacerbate the scenario such as the motherboard failing after the memory is installed.

The only two possible exceptions are:

1) A retrofit (not upgrade) of a business critical machine in an attempt to keep it alive long enough for its replacement to come on line.

2) We have explained our position to the client and the client is willing to pay for the time to find the correct parts, plus all time for installation and troubleshooting of issues arising from that installation.

It is highly unlikely that any one client would ever be so endeared to a machine that they would select option 2.

Documentation

All hardware must have a Machine Specifications ("Machine Spec") sheet filled out and placed in the The Network Documentation Binder (see Volume Four in this series).

All licenses, software, warranties, and hardware registration information should be documented in the Network Documentation Binder and in the PSA system (under "configurations").

Storage

For every machine (server, desktop, printer, firewall, etc.) there is a pouch-type folder. If there is physical media for an application, it is stored in a folder for the machine on which it is installed. The same is true of warranty and license information.

If there is electronic media, such as a downloaded application or update, those files must be saved in either the C:\!Tech or the D:\!Tech directory. See Volume Two, Chapter Twenty-Nine regarding the !Tech Directory.

Copyright © 2014 Karl W. Palachuk

The Most Important Process

The most important process regarding software and hardware is that it should be registered to the email address

Administrator@[client_domain].com.

If a human name is absolutely required, you can enter in the primary contact. But the email must be the administrator account for the client's domain.

Sometimes we think the primary contact will always be there. Maybe it's the owner. But time and time again, something happens so that the email changes, the company gets bought, the contact gets another job, etc. It is therefore critical that software (warrantees, etc.) be registered to an email address that you will always have access to. That way, you will always be able to deal with renewals or other issues, even if the primary contact is on vacation or gets hit by a bus.

All registration information must be recorded in the Network Documentation Binder and in the PSA system.

Implementation Notes

Implementing these policies follows a familiar pattern. First you need to decide on your policies. Then you need to write up your policies. After that, you'll meet with your staff and make sure they understand your policies.

These processes include policies on how you register software and hardware; storing physical media; storing electronic media; upgrade policies; and more. Don't think that this is a simple little policy. These inter-related policies affect sales and long-term goals as well as simple documentation.

Copyright © 2014 Karl W. Palachuk

When you have properly registered and documented software and hardware for your clients, you provide them with much more than the basic "proof" of ownership. When properly documented and stored, you'll have everything you need to recover or replace the client's systems in case of flood, fire, theft, or some other insurance-related incident. In fact, you'll have documentation you can fax right to the insurance company. For licenses, you'll save the client thousands of dollars because you won't have to re-buy licenses for damaged or stolen machines.

Over the long run, having all of this information properly registered will make upgrades easier to manage.

It will also make it easier for you to "retire" old equipment without leaving all kinds of software and paperwork behind. Because everything related to a specific machine is where it belongs, and where you can find it, cleaning up is easy.

It's very cool to donate old machines to a charity and include all the relevant paperwork and documentation!

As you can see, this simple-sounding process works its way into a great deal of the smooth operation of your business. Over the long run, this will make both your business and your client's business run more smoothly and profitably.

Copyright © 2014 Karl W. Palachuk

3 and 3

Three Take-Aways from This Chapter:

1. Be one of the "good guys" and put all of the client's purchases in their name!

2. Use the administrator email address for all client registrations. That way it is always available no matter what personnel changes happen down the road.

3. Keep track of all hardware and software information by using pouch folders that can be easily recycled with each machine.

Three Action Steps for Your Company:

1. _____

   _____

2. _____

   _____

3. _____

   _____

Copyright © 2014 Karl W. Palachuk

27

Local Docs, My Docs, and Storing Files on the Server

Where are your clients' files stored? This seems like it should be a simple question to answer. But the answer affects network security, keeping track of files, network speed, customer satisfaction, backups, disaster recovery, and more.

We have a very simple process for making most of these potential issues into non-issues.

Overview

In the good old days, there was a network operating system called Novell. It worked great for what it did. It really made the modern era of servers and workstations possible. In the days when the Novell ruled the world, there was a primary share on the server (for example, the i: drive or g: drive) and all client data was stored within that.

For example:

i:\

i:\Marketing

i:\Marketing\Current

i:\Marketing\old

Copyright © 2014 Karl W. Palachuk

i:\Sales

i:\Sales\Current

i:\users\Past_Campaigns

i:\users\Bob

i:\users\Bob\personal

i:\users\Denise

i:\users\Frank

i:\users\haley

i:\users\john

i:\users\Leona

i:\users\Nancy

i:\users\Preston

i:\users\Robert

i:\users\Ted

i:\users\Vicky

At some point, Windows NT began taking over the world. Then Microsoft introduced one of the most cumbersome and ridiculous schemes ever invented to lose data, bloat backups, and create a complete layer of management that was previously unheard of: The "My Documents Folder" - and, worse, the redirection of My Documents to the server!

Very simply, this is one of the stupidest things ever.

I think it's another example of Operating System envy with Apple.

Copyright © 2014 Karl W. Palachuk

Somebody somewhere came up with the concept that users are too stoopid to manage their own data. They can't know where it "really" is ... it should just **be there**. That's fine, if you want to do that on your home computer or you have no server. But in a business environment, it is perfectly okay to know where your data are located, how much there is, and who should have access to it.

Those in favor of redirecting My Documents to the server say, "You can just take care of this with AD and GP." That sounds great in theory. But there's still some hassle involved in setting up group policies. And there have been problems from time to time with file redirection and offline files. So it's not trouble-free maintenance.

We have a simple policy: Our clients don't use "my documents" and we don't redirect my docs to the server. Period. End of story.

The primary reason for this is NOT that it can have problems. The truth is, those problems are rare. The primary reason is that **Clients are HORRIBLE at managing data**. The secondary reason is that clients have low tolerance for the slow networks they create with their bad habits.

- Clients synch their video cameras and digital cameras with My Docs.

- Clients sometimes protect themselves by saving an entire copy of their C: drive to My Documents.

- Clients make backups of backups of backups. Some do this and then get loss in the catacombs they created, so they end up using a backup as the actual "live" source files.

- Clients store their MP3's in "documents" instead of "music" as soon as they learn you've excluded "music" from the files being synchronized to the server.

- Clients do weird stuff if you let them.

Copyright © 2014 Karl W. Palachuk

Then they never log off at night because logging ON in the morning takes 97 minutes. They don't know why. It's not their job to know why. But since they never log off and they never log on, they also never get a complete synch. So their mission-critical database is never copied to the server. It's never backed up. And if something goes wrong, they will never see it again.

So we don't let them do that.

Implementation Notes

Our basic policy is very straight forward:

1) All company data is stored on the server, in an appropriate folder

2) Desktops are not backed up unless the client requests it

3) If you have something on your desktop and you don't store it on the server, then we assume it is not important and we will not worry about it if there's a disaster recovery

4) Sensitive data (such as finances or personnel) will be in specific folders on the server with security assigned by appropriate groups

5) If users need folders, we will create them. BUT our very strong preference is that data be in an appropriate folder open to everyone in the appropriate group.

   Companies should operate based on the roles people fill, not on the people who fill the roles.

6) On extremely rare occasions, there are files that must exist on a specific machine. These are copied to the server each night using a tool such as Robocopy.

This policy has an advantage in that users are free to have "their stuff" on the local machine and not affect the business. At the same time, you can create a place for "their business stuff" on the server.

Benefits

One of the biggest advantages of avoiding the My Documents tangle is that profiles are easy to move during migrations. See *The Network Migration Workbook* for discussions about moving profiles . . . and taking the migration opportunity to move data off the desktops and on to the server where it belongs.

Our experience is that clients really don't care where their data is. That's why they're horrible data managers. It's not important to them. So, putting it on the server in standard directories actually allows you to work with one key employee to manage their data, archive as necessary, and develop a backup strategy that makes sense.

More and more, we want to have systems that use the desktop as a simple access device. In other words, if any desktop computer goes down, the user should be able to log onto any other workstation and just pick up where they left off. That's NOT going to happen if they rely on a roaming profile to synchronize 30 GB of data, 99% of which is totally irrelevant to the job they're doing today.

If we have to manage mini data farms all over the office because people have mission critical files on their desktops, that adds security concerns and backup concerns to the desktop maintenance. Everything's easier, faster, and more secure if we manage it on the server.

Copyright © 2014 Karl W. Palachuk

Forms

There are no specific forms for implementing this SOP. At the end of Volume Four we cover backups in some detail. There are forms for that. In this case, you just need to write up a nice policy based on the points outlined above.

You should have a discussion with your key contact about moving data to "where it belongs" on the server, backing it up, etc. We like to start this conversation with the phrase "We like to see . . .." That's a powerful tool.

"We like to see . . ." tells your client that you've thought about this. It gives the impression that you've got a standard operating procedure that works. It gives you the confidence to talk in confident terms of about how you can protect the client's data.

Try it. You'll like it.

3 and 3

Three Take-Aways from This Chapter:

1. Store data based on roles (finance, service, admin, etc.) rather than based on the individuals who play those roles.

2. All company data should be in folders on the server within a primary folder/directory.

3. Look for an opportunity to touch each computer at a new client and get their data moved to the server share and out of My Documents.

Three Action Steps for Your Company:

1. _____

   _____

2. _____

   _____

3. _____

   _____

Copyright © 2014 Karl W. Palachuk

Copyright © 2014 Karl W. Palachuk

28

Moving a Client Office

Helping a Client Move Their Office?

What's the worst way to make a major move? Without planning!

As a rule, we don't do a lot of client moves (helping a client move from one office to another). So we may not have a good checklist for moves. To be honest, we don't have a "real" checklist. But we have a long list of general guidelines for our project manager.

The keys to success in helping your client move are:

- Have as much knowledge as possible at every stage

- Make sure everything you do is in a service request (you'll create more than one)

- Plan everything as much as you can

You obviously want to make money on this job. Well, unless you bid a flat fee and let the project get completely out of control, you should make good money. So that shouldn't be an issue. Adds, moves, and changes are not included in our managed service agreements. And a move is a move.

Given that you're going to make money, you can turn your attention to helping your client have a very positive experience during a very

Copyright © 2014 Karl W. Palachuk

stressful time. The more you can do your job professionally and flawlessly, the more you'll shine when it's all over.

As you can see from the checklist below, there are LOTS of details that need your attention. That means you might have a fair bit of stress as well. You reduce that stress by planning as much as you can as far in advance as you can. And as with all things technical, the more pieces of the puzzle you control, the smoother you can make everything work.

Sometimes events are out of your control. But it is extremely rare that an office move has no planning and no advance notice. In fact, it is much more likely that an office move will involve a "build-out" of the new location. That means changes to electrical and network wiring. It means adding an internet connection.

All of that adds up to **time** so you can do some planning.

Here's a checklist of things to consider the next time you help a client move. This checklist is included in the downloadable material for this book.

1. As soon as possible

- Meet with the client to define what they need from you, schedules, and budget

- Determine how involved you will be

  o You probably want to price yourself out of the business of helping with non-technical stuff. As a rule, moving assistance is a lot cheaper than tech support, so you won't get away with $150/hr.

Copyright © 2014 Karl W. Palachuk

- o   If you cover vendor management in your managed service contract, which vendors will you take charge of?

- o   If you take on additional vendor management, who will you be working with (e.g., copier company, security company)?

- o   Make a list of all the services you are willing to perform or manage. This includes I.T. and other services such as managing subcontractors for waste management, janitorial, security systems, etc.

- Create a Service Ticket to verify that all client documentation is up to date. It should be, but we're all human. If you are familiar with the project module of your PSA, you might use that as well.

- If you have servers that are visible from the outside world (email, web server, ftp server, media server, etc.), create a service request **for each server**. Determine how you will minimize downtime. Get new IP addresses as soon as you can. Consider if this is a good time to move some services to the Cloud.

  - o   If possible, separate these moves from the big office move. It is not always possible, but it's a great idea if you can do it.

- Create a master contact list for the move. This includes names, cell phone numbers, and email addresses for everyone involved in the move:

  - o   Your key team members

  - o   Your client's key team members

Copyright © 2014 Karl W. Palachuk

    o   Phone company contact

    o   Internet Service Provider(s)

    o   Line of Business software support

    o   All other vendors (copy machines, voicemail, cabling, electrical, moving service, waste management, etc.)

    o   All key software and hardware companies who might assist with anything on the server, desktops, or network equipment

- Agree on the move date

2. One to four weeks before the move

- When will the new Internet connection go in?

  (Who is the new ISP? If not the same as old, which services need to be moved as well? Will we be coordinating the installation and managing the vendor on this?)

- This is a great opportunity to upgrade the client firewall. A firewall that's just a few years old will not handle the new higher speeds available today.

- This is a great opportunity to upgrade the client switch(es) as well. Ideally, you will install all-Gigabit or even 10 GB switches. Many offices have Gigabit NICs on all of their computers, but have mostly 100 Mb switches.

- Test all battery backups. Because they tend to be purchased in batches, they also tend to fail in batches. Plan to buy new equipment for the new office and do not move bad equipment.

Copyright © 2014 Karl W. Palachuk

- Once you know how much equipment will be in the new server room (including phone systems, security systems, etc.), verify that you have sufficient battery backups for all equipment.

- Ask your primary client contact to review warranties and service contracts for all equipment (Network equipment, servers, desktops, laptops, copiers, printers, etc.). Have them verify that warranties are not voided if someone other than the vendors moves the equipment.

- If you can be involved in selecting the wiring room/server room, that would be ideal. More likely, there's already a room selected. You should make sure it has adequate electricity. That means at least one or two isolated 30-amp circuits with four outlets each. There should be adequate ventilation for the amount of equipment in use.

- If you can be involved in the network wiring, that's good as well. Even if you don't do the wiring, encourage the client to get at least two drops per workstation. I like to encourage them to put the outlets about 36-42 inches off the floor so they're accessible. That's just me. Cat6 is now standard.

- To the extent possible, work with the cabling folks to make sure that network connections are labeled on each end (server room and at the wall plate).

- When wiring is completed, post a wiring map with network drop numbers. This is very handy for many pieces of the move/set up.

- If you handle phones, audit the lines in use and eliminate any that are no longer needed. If the move is due to growth or expansion, make sure the new site has enough lines and equipment to handle the load (and expected growth).

Copyright © 2014 Karl W. Palachuk

- As you acquire new equipment (router, firewall, new PCs, etc.), be certain that everything is set up properly and documented. There's no point starting "behind" in the documentation process.

- If you need to build equipment racks or shelves, do this in the week before the move. If possible, do it at the new location. If not, do what you can to assemble them at the old office so they can be moved and assembled quickly at the new location.

- Design the new network the way you want it to be. That means you review your company's IP Address Allocation policy (see Chapter 37) and set up the new network accordingly

- Verify that you are getting good backups every night (or whatever your schedule is). Keep verifying this every day. Really. You cannot take a chance that you'll have a glitch at this critical time. That is what managed service is about.

- Determine the locations for network printers, scanners, time card machines, video cameras, and any other equipment that touches the new network at the new office

- Create Service Requests. That's multiple. Create a few service requests – one for each area of responsibility you take on. Do not create just one SR and call it "Help with move." For example, you might have one for managing the I.T. move, one for configuring the new network, one for take down/set up of equipment, and one for fine-tuning after the move. If you are familiar with the project module of your PSA, you might use that as well.

- Prepare memos for your primary contact and all users. Explain what you'll be doing, when you expect to do it, and let them know what you expect from THEM. Do not rely on your contact to spread the word. She's overwhelmed with all the other details. You own this process; you own the communication.

- If there are more desktops than you can set up and test in a day, hire temps or recruit folks from your local I.T. Pro user group. Make sure you have enough help!

- Create a checklist for every single thing that must be done at each desktop when you set it up at the new location.

- Create a master checklist of every single piece of equipment you expect to touch. This includes network equipment, servers, desktops, laptops, cameras, copy machines, printers, etc. Everything. This list will be printed out and used to keep track of the successful configuration and testing of every single device on the day of the move.

3. On the Day Before and Day of The Move

(Very often, the actual move begins the day before. Sometimes it begins when work ends at 5 PM. Other times, it begins at 8 AM the day before so there's plenty of time for everyone to pack up their office.

- Arrange to have each user shut down and unplug everything from their desktop computer. Work with your contact to get everyone a moving box or paper file box for their desk. All of their computer-related stuff goes in that box. In this way, each person keeps their keyboard, mouse, speakers, wires, etc. Make sure they put their name on the box!

- At the new office you and your team re-assemble all computers. Do not encourage or let end-users do this. Make

Copyright © 2014 Karl W. Palachuk

sure you have a plan for how you will handle the situation if a machine fails to start up at the new office.

- If you have the personnel to do so, assign one person to have primary responsibility for the network (firewall, switches, server, etc.), one person primary responsibility for the desktops and laptops, and one person in charge of tackling all the little weird stuff that comes up. The most technically competent person should be on the network, the next most competent should be on fighting fires, and the rest of the team should be on desktops.

- At the new location on day of setup, your project lead should show up at 8:00 AM and verify what's going on, where the equipment is, and generally get ready for the day. You'll be amazed at what can happen at this moment: No Internet; no electricity; all the desktop machines dumped in the conference room; network wiring is 50% complete; your primary contact will be an hour late; none of the monitors have arrived yet from the old location; and so forth. Therefore . . .

- Schedule your team to arrive at 9:00 AM or even 10:00 AM. That gives you time to make sure everything's ready, and what additional chores need to be added to the list in order to be successful today.

- Before the desktop team arrives, Fine Tune the Checklist. That means you set up one machine and go through every single step in order. If you left something blank, it needs to be filled in here. For example, if you did not settle on an IP configuration at the time the checklist was created, you need to fill that in now. Make any necessary changes to the checklist and then print a copy for each workstation.

Copyright © 2014 Karl W. Palachuk

- You are not responsible for testing all electrical outlets in the new office. But you should take responsibility of the outlets you plug equipment into. Test all power outlets using a tester like the one pictured here. You can buy this for $5 at Home Depot. Even with a UPS, you want to plug equipment into a good outlet.

All you need to do is to plug this device into an electrical socket. The pattern of LED lights will tell you whether you have an open ground, open neutral, or open hot. It will also tell you if the hot and ground wires are reversed, and if the hot and neutral wires are reversed. And of course it will tell you if the wiring is correct. Repeat this process for every outlet you use.

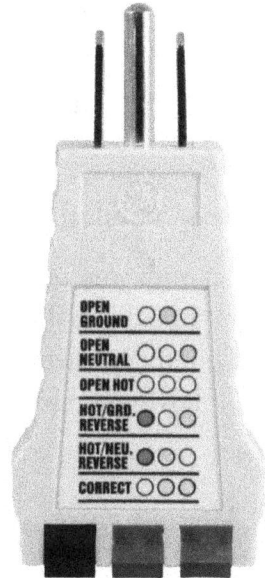

- When you think you're finished, test the server and network equipment at the new site

    o Verify firewalls are properly configured

    o Verify that you can access the Internet

    o Verify that all servers are working properly, have no errors in the event logs, can reach the internet, can print, and all services are started

    o Verify that all network printers are working

    o Verify that all other network-connected devices are working properly

- When you think you're finished, test the desktops/laptops at the new site

    o Verify that all computers can access the Internet

    o Verify that all computers can connect to file shares, print, and both send and receive email to an outside address

    o If you're involved with the phones, verify that the desktop telephone is working

Note on Physically Moving Equipment

Check with your insurance agent, but my advice is that you and your team should actually **move nothing**. You can take machines apart and put them together. But all moving should be done by the client or their moving company. Do not take on that responsibility.

4. After the move

- Plan on having someone onsite the first full workday after the move. Ideally, this person will have a few unrelated service tickets to work. They should just "be around" enough to fix little issues that arise, but they should be doing productive work rather than just waiting around.

- Verify that all documentation is up to spec. That means new equipment is documented on site in the Network Documentation Binder and in your PSA. If configurations changed on old equipment, their documentation needs to be updated. New network IP schemes need to be documented, etc. Everything. Everything. Everything.

- Agree with the client on how old, unused, broken, and obsolete equipment will be handled. You might help them donate it to charity, take it to the recycling center, or sell it on Ebay. Make a plan. If the job is big, this might be a separate service request.

Concluding Comments

No matter how small the office, a move is a major project. It will have lots of stress from various stakeholders. Your team needs to be the calmest, best prepared, and most professional people on the job throughout this process. In times of stress, people naturally gravitate to those who appear the most calm and collected.

Remember: Something will go wrong. You don't know what it is or how big of a problem it is. But you'll find, fix it, and move on. It could be really big. With luck, it will be really small.

Copyright © 2014 Karl W. Palachuk

3 and 3

Three Take-Aways from This Chapter:

1. Your preparation will dramatically reduce the stress level of your primary contact.

2. This is the perfect time to bring all documentation up to spec. Your new network should be perfectly documented.

3. Try to plan as far in advance as possible so that you minimize unexpected costs. The client may be too busy to notice that you are doing this, so feel free to tell them.

Three Action Steps for Your Company:

1. _____

   _____

2. _____

   _____

3. _____

   _____

Copyright © 2014 Karl W. Palachuk

Section IV

Practical How-To Examples

Copyright © 2014 Karl W. Palachuk

Copyright © 2014 Karl W. Palachuk

29

Troubleshooting Guidelines

Eight Rules and Thirteen Techniques for Success

Troubleshooting is a very interesting piece of our jobs. It is almost never taught. Yet it is central to our success. After all, if you have no troubleshooting skills, you'll spend lots of time NOT solving problems. Eventually, you'll go do something else for a living. Conversely, the better you are at troubleshooting, the faster you solve problems and the more money you make.

So . . . you guessed it . . . you should have some standard training on troubleshooting. There are three keys to success with troubleshooting. Two of them can be taught. First, there are *rules* or *principles of operation*. If you can follow the rules, they will help you make good decisions. Second, there are *specific techniques* to follow. We use some techniques for one occasion and other techniques for other occasions.

The third element can't be taught: *Experience*. Experience is the magic ingredient. How do you know which rules apply? How do you know which technique to use? In fact, how do you know exactly what to do without troubleshooting at all? Because you've seen it before. You've done the task many times. You've solved similar problems. And if you're good at applying rules and techniques, then experience just makes you faster and better.

Copyright © 2014 Karl W. Palachuk

This article focuses on the skills you can teach. These can be imparted to your technicians. And many of the rules are designed specifically to save your company money. The most obvious example of this is the rule to call for help after 60 minutes with no progress.

Note: This chapter goes hand-in-hand with the next chapter: *Troubleshooting and Repair Logs*. We will use this and refer to it as the TSR Log.

A training on troubleshooting is useful so that everyone on your team takes a similar approach, and because they can learn from each other. The only way anyone gets the experience that will make them great at troubleshooting is to spend time troubleshooting!

Sometimes you go into a troubleshooting situation from the start. For example, something is not working and you are going to find out why. At other times an issue becomes a troubleshooting situation. In other words, you went in to do one thing and ended up finding a bigger problem than you thought.

The only real difference between these two situations is your level of awareness going in. Troubleshooting rules and techniques are not different. The biggest problem with a situation that becomes a troubleshooting job is that you might not realize you've slipped into troubleshooting mode for some time. That's why one of the rules is to ask for help if you're not making progress.

Interestingly enough, troubleshooting experience in other areas can be very helpful in troubleshooting computers and networks. If you fix anything (cars, toasters, etc.), you'll see that many rules and techniques apply to other fields. Now let's look at rules and techniques for troubleshooting IT issues.

Eight Rules for Troubleshooting Hardware, Software, and Networks

Copyright © 2014 Karl W. Palachuk

1. Try the obvious solution first.

There's a famous quote in medicine: "When you hear hoof beats behind you, don't expect to see a zebra." (Dr. Theodore Woodward, University of Maryland School of Medicine). That means you should not start by looking for weird problems.

2. Document everything.

Use the TSR Log!!! A TSR log must be started at the 1 hour point of any single ongoing issue. Documentation also means that you label everything you can. Seriously: this helps. A perfect example is hard drives. Before you start switching hard drives around, make sure you label them so you keep track of where you started and what you did.

3. Only change one thing at a time.

Inexperienced technicians (and many clients) make several changes at once. For example, they apply all the waiting updates, switch out the network cable, and change the IP properties. The obvious problem (whether the issue is fixed or not) is that you have no way of knowing which change made a difference.

In addition, one of these changes alone may have changed behavior that you can measure and document. That knowledge might be useful if the issue is not solved because you could have eliminated two of those, but now you can't eliminate any of them.

This rule is extremely important. In fact, it's the reason we do not allow clients to take on two major projects at the same time, such as a network migration and changing ISPs. If you have network issues and you've changed two things system wide, you can spend a lot of time chasing the rabbit down the wrong hole.

Copyright © 2014 Karl W. Palachuk

4. Know what you know.

You should be completely and honestly aware of the margins of your knowledge. In addition, this rule affects documentation. As you progress, you need to be very clear about solutions you have tried and eliminated from consideration. This keeps you from trying the same thing again and again. Volume Four of this series has two chapters on working with third party tech support and documenting calls.

5. Don't forget the basics!

Even experienced technicians forget this one. If they think they know what the problem is about, they jump in and try a few things. A half hour later, they call someone else on the team who asks "What kind of errors are in the event logs?" Uh . . .. If you haven't checked the event logs, you might be embarrassed to see that the problem is obvious.

While writing this book I heard a familiar buzz from a computer in the office. I dutifully bought two different size fans so I could replace the culprit no matter its size. After replacing the fan, the problem persisted. I traced the problem by shutting office equipment one at a time until I discovered the real issue: a loose speaker cable causing an electrical buzz. Duh.

6. Slow down, get more done.

I've covered this many times in my blog and my books. There are several angles to this rule. If you're in a hurry, you won't be careful, you'll miss things, you'll forget the other rules, and you'll become

Copyright © 2014 Karl W. Palachuk

frustrated faster. Go slow. Ask for help. Splash water on your face. Take your lunch break. Get a fresh pair of eyes.

7. Use your PSA's knowledgebase capability!

Your professional services automation tool is a great place to document issues so you can do research within your own knowledgebase. Has your team solved similar problems? Is there a hotfix already downloaded to the cloud drive? Don't duplicate work of any kind, even research.

8. Ask for help!

You're not alone. The maximum time anyone should work on any problem before stopping and calling for feedback or support is 60 minutes. It is critical to the company's profit to not waste time by continually trying the same thing over and over or to simply stumble around hoping to find success.

The first time I took a vacation and handed my clients over to an employee, I told him that he is not alone. He can call HP, Microsoft, Dell, Symantec, me, other technicians, or anyone else who might be able to help. Sometimes a vendor knows the answer but the online support system is horrible. Or the vendor has undocumented fixes that they only hand out if you call in with the specific problem. At other times, another tech will have worked on something similar. Or they might just suggest a different approach.

The more consistently you apply these rules, the smoother your operation will work. One of the great benefits of experience is that you take note of "weird stuff" you come across. Having a good process

Copyright © 2014 Karl W. Palachuk

will help you isolate the weird stuff, document it, and add it to your internal mental database.

These rules are like your muscles of success. You need to practice them so you'll get good enough that they become an automatic part of your troubleshooting process.

Thirteen Techniques for Troubleshooting Hardware, Software, and Networks

Techniques are different from the rules above. Rules are big-picture guidelines. Techniques are specific approaches or actions you use to find problems and isolate solutions. Everything above continues to apply. Here are some techniques you will employ in troubleshooting. If you've been in technology long, you'll recognize all of them, even if you didn't have labels for them.

The wisdom of an experienced troubleshooter is to know which technique to attempt first, second, etc. Some techniques are opposites of each other. Experience will help you decide how to start and how to proceed.

1. Start with the highest probability.

This is simply the action that executes Rule #1 above. But remember that things change over time. Here's an incredibly general but accurate example:

Let's say there's a problem with the network. Period. That's all you know. In the world of Windows NT 4.0, I would say to start with the physical connection (cable, NIC, switch). In the days of Windows 2011/2012 I would say to start with DNS. One of the jokes in my office is "All problems are DNS." That's surprisingly helpful!

Copyright © 2014 Karl W. Palachuk

2. Start with the Physical.

This technique is as old as networking. But it also applies to software and hardware issues. For example, if a hard drive is old or beginning to die, it might spend an excessive amount of time writing and re-writing data, marking bad sectors, and moving things around.

We tend to forget this technique today because hardware (and networking) has become extremely reliable. The network-specific equivalent of this rule is "Work your way up the stack." Remember the ISO (Open Systems Interconnection) model? The stack looks like this:

Layer 7. Application

Layer 6. Presentation

Layer 5. Session

Layer 4. Transport

Layer 3. Network

Layer 2. Data link

Layer 1. Physical

3. Start with the program. This is the opposite of Technique #2. Assume that cabling, network, and connections are all stable. This technique is actually more common today than #2. You examine the program, then the operating system, and on down.

One great place to start with any program is the log files. That's where errors get reported. The log files give you lots of information about what's working and what's not. You just have to go look at them.

Copyright © 2014 Karl W. Palachuk

4. Apply all the patches, fixes, and updates.

It is amazing how many problems go away when you apply all the patches to the hardware, operating system, and program. Keep updating until there's nothing left to add. Now test the issue. Very often, the problem will be gone. You might be dissatisfied that you don't know what caused or fixed the problem. See the last technique, below.

5. What has changed?

Whether changed by the client, automatic updates, or even one of your staff, changes are a very frequent cause of problems. This is an easy technique to try: Simply reverse the change if you can. Often you cannot. In such cases, you simply have to find the new conflict and figure out how to solve the problem. But at least you're on the right track.

6. Order matters.

Sometimes a problem only happens because a series of actions was taken in a specific order. Change the order and you have no problem. This is the most common cause of people saying that a problem is "random." If there's one thing a computer system is NOT, it's not random. This is why it is critical to get clients to report exactly what happened. In what order did they open programs, save files, etc.?

7. Serial substitution.

This means that you change one thing and test. If the problem is not solved, change that thing back. Then change the next thing. If the problem is not solved, change that back. And so forth. The technique

Copyright © 2014 Karl W. Palachuk

works best when you can define the possible variables. For example, in TCP/IP you have the IP address, subnet mast, default gateways, hosts file, DNS, and so forth. You can literally make a list and check things one by one. Documentation is critical to this. Use the TSR log!

8. Troubleshooting Checklists.

We get frustrated when we call tech support for a client and the ISP wants us to verify that the router is plugged in, the cables are good, etc. But we have some checklists ourselves. After all, if a client called you and said that her computer doesn't start, you'd go down your own checklist. Is the UPS plugged in? Is the light red or green?

Creating a few simple checklists can help your technicians to quickly solve some of the most basic problems. This helps them learn troubleshooting and saves you money!

9. Reproduce the problem.

This is particularly helpful with intermittent issues. Can you (or the client) reproduce the problem every time? If so, that will give you great clues about where to start. If not, then you need to begin investigating when the problem happens, which programs are being used, and so forth.

10. Have users help with documentation.

This follows from Technique #9. If you can't re-create an intermittent problem on demand, then you need to engage the client to help you. Give them a form with instructions. When the problem recurs, they need to tell you what were they doing, which programs were open, etc. Anything they can give you at that very moment may be helpful.

Copyright © 2014 Karl W. Palachuk

They can either keep a paper log, enter notes in the service ticket, or email information to you.

11. Do you have multiple problems?

This is essentially the opposite of Technique #1. It will certainly not be the first thing you consider. But at some point, consider the possibility that two things changed, or two things failed at the same time. It does happen. Finding one issue may or may not help to find the other issue. But fixing one issue will usually make the other issue easier to find!

12. Product-specific gotchas.

This technique relies heavily on experience. Sometimes you just "know" that a program behaves a certain way, or comes set up wrong out of the box, or you have to connect a certain cable first. This is knowledge that doesn't really help much with figuring out problems generally.

But whenever you see one specific product, you know what you need to do. This is also one of the reasons that you will be more profitable is you have a small set or products you sell. You get to know those products and can troubleshoot them very quickly.

13. Do you care why?

This is a completely different approach. Do you care why the problem happened? Can you simply reboot and fix it? Can you roll back the system to the last restore point and it works? As left-brained techno-goobers, we want to understand what happened. But as business

Copyright © 2014 Karl W. Palachuk

owners and managers, that may not be the most important question. If you can fix something quickly, who cares why it broke?

Note: If the problem happens again, then you need to care. If the problem recurs, then you need to pick the right technique and troubleshoot the problem until you really fix it.

Remember: Computers are not random. That makes troubleshooting them a very systematic job. Unless you've engaged a random function, computers always do exactly the same thing under that same circumstances. When that does not appear to be true, it's because you haven't explored enough to determine when it does one thing and when it does another.

What remains true under all circumstances is that the rules always apply, and one of these techniques will reveal the solution. There's very little you can do to speed up experience except to tackle as many problems as possible.

Copyright © 2014 Karl W. Palachuk

3 and 3

Three Take-Aways from This Chapter:

1. Successful troubleshooting relies on rules or principles of operation, specific techniques, and experience. The first two can be taught. Experience can only be acquired.

2. When working with younger technicians, take a troubleshooting frame of mind and explain to them why you do what you do.

3. Implement rules about getting help – and follow them yourself.

Three Action Steps for Your Company:

1. _____

   _____

2. _____

   _____

3. _____

   _____

Copyright © 2014 Karl W. Palachuk

30

Troubleshooting and Repair Logs

At several places in this four-book series I have mentioned the **TSR Log** or Troubleshooting and Repair log. The TSR Log is an extremely valuable tool for tracking issues, working with tech support from vendors, and documenting your work. We use a TSR Log whenever we build a server, when we call any vendor, and when a tech has worked on any issue for more than 30 minutes without making progress.

For newer technicians, we might require a TSR Log for any issue that causes more than 15 minutes work without progress.

In addition to being a GREAT documentation tool, the TSR Log is a great way to learn troubleshooting. It forces the user into thinking rigorously and documenting in such a way that you can effectively seek assistance from your co-workers or "tech support" on the other end of the phone.

Overview

For more than a decade I have trained my staff on a key philosophy for success: *Know What You Know*. One of the important tools you have to help in this endeavor is the TSR Log. With a TSR Log, you can state very clearly what you've tried and what the results were. You can make a change and then undo it with confidence because you

Copyright © 2014 Karl W. Palachuk

have a map of where you've been. This is perfect for working with a manager, another technician, or a vendor.

If you own the *Network Migration Workbook*, you'll find a sample TSR Log in each of the checklists. We use a TSR Log every time we build a new server. It's great documentation . . . and more.

If anything goes wrong, you'll be able to document exactly what happened and where it happened in the process. This is very handy if you find yourself rebuilding that server from scratch someday. You're going to hit the same snag and it will be very handy to have quick access to the solution.

A TSR Log helps you keep very accurate information about how long it actually takes to build a server. This number will change over time as you gain experience and Microsoft releases updates. But even though this is a bit of a moving target, the more accurate your information, the more profitable you can make your next migration! (This is true because your time estimates will be more accurate.)

As we learned in the last chapter, we need to make sure that we're not continually performing the same "fixes" again and again. If you keep track of what you've tried, in a systematic manner, you can eliminate causes for whatever problem you're troubleshooting. And when you engage outside help at the 60-minute mark, you can relay exactly what you have and have not tried. Sometimes vendors insist on going over the same ground, but you can stop them from going over the same ground more than once! Excellent records about what you've done can also help you get a problem escalated more quickly (sometimes).

And, of course, when you need to go over a problem with a client, you will have excellent records about what you did, what you didn't do, who was involved, and how long it took. This is all good information.

Copyright © 2014 Karl W. Palachuk

Implementation Notes

Implementation of this SOP is easy to initiate. But it can be difficult to get everyone on the team to go along with. Over time, you need to support one another by asking "Did you have a TSR Log?" For us, this is important enough to impact quarterly reviews. If the service manager asks to see a TSR Log and there isn't one, that's a potential career-ending incident!

First, you'll need a form (see next section). We post ours in .pdf format on our SharePoint site so technicians can access it easily. We also require technicians to carry one printed out and ready to go at all times (see Chapter Twenty-One). We require them to use a TSR Log whenever they have been "stuck" on a problem for any amount of time.

Second, to use the TSR Log, you need to simply fill out some key data and then proceed to take notes. There are two "triggers" for taking notes. One is whenever something significant happens. For example, when the server is rebooted, when a change is made, when an error occurs.

The second reason you enter something in the log is simply when you pass a fifteen-minute mark. Never let more than 15 minutes pass without an entry. It might simply be "Setup continued to unpack files." That way you know you didn't simply forget the log. But, more importantly, it will really help you pinpoint when things "go wrong" during an installation, configuration, troubleshooting, etc.

Once you have TSR Logs that have actually been used by technicians to solve problems, you'll need to deal with them properly. That means keeping all related notes together with the TSR Log. If you worked with a vendor to solve a problem, request a copy of **their notes** by

Copyright © 2014 Karl W. Palachuk

email. This is true of Microsoft, Trend, HP, or anyone else you deal with.

Over time you'll see that your notes are MUCH better than theirs! Attach a copy of those notes to this document.

When the issue is resolved, three hole punch this document and place it in the Tech Notes section of the Network Documentation Binder.

No. Having a PSA system does NOT eliminate the need for an NDB. In the PSA, annotate any related Service Tickets with a brief description of the problem and final resolution. Then simply refer to this TSR log by log number for full details on the issue.

For migration projects and server builds, you should probably keep a photocopy of the TSR Log in a file cabinet at your office. You can file by client/date, or simply keep all TSR logs together in one file drawer. Just make sure you can find it if you need it later.

Form

The TSR Log has three sections. At the top are sections for the client and the vendor (if relevant). After that, you simply need a series of lines with a place for date stamps and a line for notes.

There's no great mystery here. But a sample TSR Log is included in the downloadable material for this book.

Copyright © 2014 Karl W. Palachuk

The TSR Log

Section One: Client

- Client _____
- Date _____
- Contact _____
- Technician _____
- Phone _____
- Log # _____

(The Log Number should be created as follows: Year.month.day.issue # i.e. 2014.07.08.01)

- Description of Issue

Section Two: Vendor

- Support Service _____
- Required Numbers or Codes _____
- SR(X) _____
- Phone Number _____
- Service Contract _____
- Date and Time Initiated _____

Copyright © 2014 Karl W. Palachuk

Section Three: Notes

_____:_____ _____

_____:_____ _____

_____:_____ _____

(repeat)

Final Notes

If you're not used to TSR Logs, or rigorous note-taking, this one might be difficult to execute. But stick with it and everyone on the team will get better at some of the most important things you do.

Remember: Most of your LOST labor comes from re-work and disorganized troubleshooting. TSR Logs can help you address both of those issues.

We all know that computers don't act randomly. They can't. So when someone says that errors occur "randomly," they can't be correct. There's a pattern or a cause. We just can't see it.

With TSR Logs, we have a good chance of finding the pattern – and solving the problem – a lot faster!

Copyright © 2014 Karl W. Palachuk

3 and 3

Three Take-Aways from This Chapter:

1. Start a TSR Log whenever you work on any issue for 60 minutes without resolution.

2. When you start using TSR Logs, review them together as a team. Discuss what's good and what might change. They're also great for reviewing problems with clients. And great fodder for staff training.

3. File your TSR Logs so you can find them again. More than once you'll come back years later to access this resource . . . IF you have it to refer to.

Three Action Steps for Your Company:

1. _____

   _____

2. _____

   _____

3. _____

   _____

Copyright © 2014 Karl W. Palachuk

Copyright © 2014 Karl W. Palachuk

31

HIPAA Part One - Training

The next three chapters address HIPAA – The Health Insurance Portability and Accountability Act. If you work with "covered entities" such as doctors or insurance companies, then having some HIPAA policies could be a very profitable piece of your IT consulting business.

Background

HIPAA has been largely ignored by small businesses since it was passed in the mid 1990's. The Privacy Rule of HIPAA was published in 2000 and modified several times since then. Major revisions were implemented in 2013 and final enforcement became effective in September of 2013.

Under this rule, doctors, insurance companies, and other healthcare providers are "Covered Entities."

You come into the picture because you are a "Business Associate" under the Privacy Rule. A Business Associate is someone who performs services for a Covered Entity and may have access to individually identifiable patient health information. A Business Associate may also be someone who works for or with another Business Associate and has access to individually identifiable patient health information.

Copyright © 2014 Karl W. Palachuk

For example:

- Doctor Doolittle is a Covered Entity

- You – his managed service provider – are a Business Associate of Dr. D.

- The company you work with to provide offsite backup services is a Business Associate of you

You are most directly affected by the HITECH Act (Health Information Technology for Economic and Clinical Health Act) associated with HIPAA. HITECH governs the security and disclosure rules around the technical side of patient records. This includes where data can be stored, how it can be stored, and the consequences of a data breach.

You must have a Business Associate Agreement in place for each Covered Entity you do business with. This is the implementation that became effective in 2013. You must also have a Business Associate Agreement in place for each Business Associate you do business with.

You need to know this stuff.

To give you some hope of understanding all this, the US Dept. of Health and Human Services (HHS) has put together a web site called HIPAA Administrative Simplification Statute and Rules – here: http://www.hhs.gov/ocr/privacy/hipaa/administrative/index.html.

You can read the complete revised Privacy Rule at the Federal Registry: http://www.gpo.gov/fdsys/pkg/FR-2013-01-25/pdf/2013-01073.pdf (138 pages).

Key action point for you: You must have your Business Associate Agreements in place ASAP!

Copyright © 2014 Karl W. Palachuk

The Three Faces of HIPAA

When we look at implementing HIPAA policies with our clients, we see three key elements: Training, Compliance, and Documentation. We'll cover a bit on training in this chapter. Chapter Thirty-Two covers compliance, which involves both assessment and remediation. Chapter Thirty-three addresses documentation. You are not HIPAA compliant until you have documented everything that makes you HIPAA compliant.

HIPAA Training

You need some HIPAA training. Whether you take a class, buy a book, or read the government web site, you need to come up to speed on this stuff – or stop servicing Covered Entities. We have a minor vertical in healthcare, so we are working on everyone's compliance rather than giving up the clients.

I took the 4Med training (http://www.4medapproved.com/).

Training is really a two-step process. First you need to get trained. Second, you should offer a bit of training for your clients. You might do the training yourself or resell a program such as 4Med.

Doctors – especially small Doctor offices – have worked very hard to ignore HIPAA as much as they can. One of the major changes in 2013 is that penalties are being handed down to smaller and smaller Covered Entities. So there are more and more stories in the news about small doctor's offices being fined large amounts of money. That will help you sell this.

Copyright © 2014 Karl W. Palachuk

In addition to that, enforcement has expanded so that state attorneys general can now enforce HIPAA compliance. That means pretty much any public agency can now be petitioned to enforce HIPAA. As a result, you'll see more and more small cases being brought up.

If you want to start gathering some examples for your newsletter or marketing materials, here are a couple of resources. First, I have started a Pinterest board about HIPAA here: http://pinterest.com/karlpalachuk/hipaa-news/.

Second, you can set up a Google Alert at www.google.com/alerts for HIPAA violations or HIPAA news and get regular emails about new information.

HIPAA training for you is not expensive – especially when you consider that it opens up a new world of opportunities to make money. Once you know the rules around HIPAA breaches and enforcement, you can sell training, assessments, remediation, and documentation. After that you can sell a managed service for HIPAA compliance maintenance. And you can market yourself against I.T. providers who are not HIPAA compliant and not able to deliver compliance services.

The Good News / Bad News

The good news for you is that there's lots of opportunity here. It's the law. It's been coming for almost 20 years. It's being enforced. Doctors, insurance companies, and other Covered Entities need you to come up to speed on HIPAA so they can be legal.

The bad news is that some doctors will simply refuse to comply. And you should fire them.

I talked to a doctor in 2013 who said that he was not worried. As far as he knows, he's fine. This conversation tool place while he was carrying a laptop from exam room to exam room filled with patient records. I asked him where his HIPAA documentation was. Of course he had none. I informed him that even if he were compliant, he's still in violation of the law if he doesn't have it documented. He shrugged it off. "They won't come after me."

Maxim to remember: You can't care more about the client's business (network) (data) than they do!

We can't have people like that as clients. We only need a tiny $50,000 fine to feel the pinch. A $500,000 fine would put us out of business.

Copyright © 2014 Karl W. Palachuk

3 and 3

Three Take-Aways from This Chapter:

1. A Business Associate is someone who performs services for a Covered Entity and may have access to individually identifiable patient health information.

2. You must have your Business Associate Agreements in place ASAP.

3. Lots of people will make money without being HIPAA compliant. But one day they will receive a fine that puts them out of business. Don't be that company.

Three Action Steps for Your Company:

1. _____

   _____

2. _____

   _____

3. _____

   _____

Copyright © 2014 Karl W. Palachuk

32

HIPAA Part Two - Compliance

For terminology in this chapter, see the last chapter, or keep a thumb in Appendix A.

On the next page is a graphic that illustrates the big stages to a great HIPAA Compliance program internally and with your clients. The last chapter talked about training and the next chapter covers documentation. This chapter covers the middle parts.

HIPAA Compliance

There are primarily four things you need to address regarding HIPAA compliance:

1) You need to become HIPAA compliant

2) You need to sign Business Associate Agreements

3) You need to develop and deliver HIPAA assessments

4) You need to help your clients become (and stay) compliant

Go.

Luckily, there are actually few requirements for small Covered Entities (doctors, etc.) and small Business Associates (you). That means it is pretty easy for them to become HIPAA compliant. The big stick that cures most potential problems is **encryption**. If a laptop is

Copyright © 2014 Karl W. Palachuk

secured and the hard drive encrypted, for example, you don't even have to report a lost laptop that contains thousands of patient records.

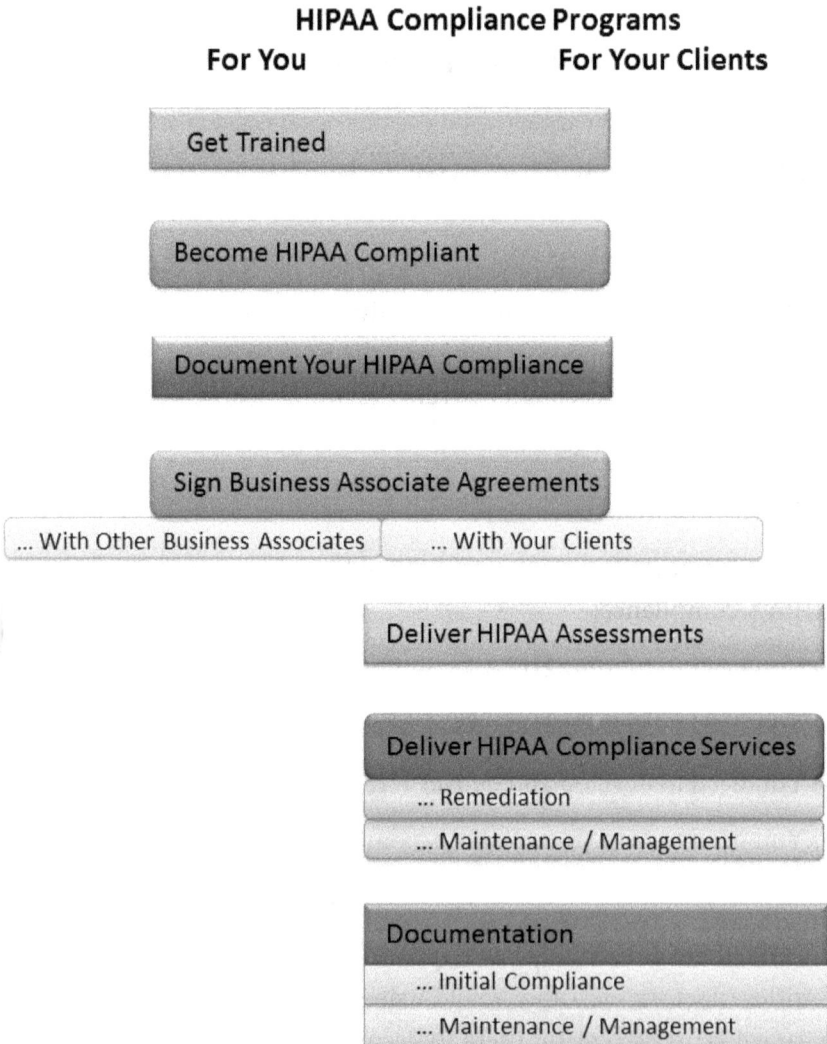

HIPAA Compliance Programs

For You   **For Your Clients**

Get Trained

Become HIPAA Compliant

Document Your HIPAA Compliance

Sign Business Associate Agreements

... With Other Business Associates   ... With Your Clients

Deliver HIPAA Assessments

Deliver HIPAA Compliance Services

... Remediation

... Maintenance / Management

Documentation

... Initial Compliance

... Maintenance / Management

Copyright © 2014 Karl W. Palachuk

Data can be in use, at rest, archived, or backed up to various media. In all cases, everything in the world of HIPAA compliance is easier if the data are encrypted. We have not, traditionally, encrypted everything at every stage. But in some cases, that will be the answer going forward.

Let's look at the four items a bit more.

1) You need to become HIPAA compliant. That means you need to develop one or more policies to document how you handle client data, training, etc. Going through this process will help you start to build HIPAA assessments and procedures for your clients.

If you don't know where to start or what you need to do, the best place to start is training. See the last chapter.

2) You need to sign Business Associate Agreements (BAAs) with all Covered Entities you have as clients and all other Business Associates you do business with. Copies of all of these should go into your HIPAA compliance file/folder/binder. Copies go into each clients' HIPAA compliance file/folder/binder and each of your BA's HIPAA compliance file/folder/binder.

There are sample BAA's on the Internet. You will also receive a sample with any good training you take. If you think this is just a huge meaningless exercise in covering your butt . . . you'd be correct. But a good BAA will address the core elements of your compliance.

Keep very good records. You need to create a binder (yes, a physical binder) and an electronic folder where you store all signed BAAs. As a service provider, this is the most important part of your HIPAA compliance: Documentation.

Copyright © 2014 Karl W. Palachuk

3) You need to develop and deliver HIPAA assessments. There's actually quite a bit of work here. And with every doctor's office you visit you'll add things to the list. So right now we're charging for the assessment because there's so much work involved. Even delivery of the assessment takes some effort because you have to document everything that doesn't need to change as well as everything that does.

The assessment should go into the client's HIPAA Compliance Binder and become both the action plan for remediation and the first draft of a report on HIPAA Compliance Documentation.

Eventually your assessment tool will be a very thorough checklist (Doesn't that sound familiar?). Part of it is based on client interviews (doctors and staff), part on observation in the office, and part on an examination of hardware, software, and data-related processes.

Please note: You probably want to deal with only the HITECH (Health Information Technology for Economic and Clinical Health Act) portion of HIPAA. You are not responsible for all HIPAA compliance because some of it has to do with the layout of the office, staff procedures, and other elements over which you probably have no control.

4) You need to help your clients become (and stay) compliant. Remediation (fixing) of problems related to record management and data services is where you excel. Once you have an assessment, you can begin to fix things.

Fixes will include documentation, processes, education, and probably changes to hardware, software, and services. Remediation might be cheap or it might be expensive, depending on the current practices and equipment.

Copyright © 2014 Karl W. Palachuk

A Few Practical Considerations

We have developed a "package" for assessing, remediating, and documenting a small medical office. Right now it's pretty expensive because we are including all labor not directly related to projects that might result from a major problem (e.g., if the server needs to be replaced altogether, that's a separate project).

If you decide you don't want to get into all this stuff, you really need to figure out what you will do with medical-related clients. At a minimum, you need to have them sign BAAs to cover YOUR butt whether they choose to be HIPAA compliant or not.

If you choose not to offer HIPAA compliance services, you should find someone who does and work out a referral or affiliate arrangement.

Copyright © 2014 Karl W. Palachuk

3 and 3

Three Take-Aways from This Chapter:

1. Encrypting data can solve lots of HIPAA compliance challenges.

2. This is an evolving area of consulting that you can get into. It will take some work, but there's huge opportunity here.

3. Document everything you do internally or with clients related to HIPAA. Make it part of your process.

Three Action Steps for Your Company:

1. _____

   _____

2. _____

   _____

3. _____

   _____

Copyright © 2014 Karl W. Palachuk

33

HIPAA Part Three - Documentation

So far we've looked at HIPAA Training and HIPAA Compliance. Now let get into HIPAA Documentation.

Documentation is the most important piece of HIPAA compliance for you and for your clients. The rules are very clear: If you do everything right and don't document it, then you are out of compliance. Luckily, the requirements for small covered entities (doctors, etc.) and business associates (you) are not overly burdensome. See the documents at the Health and Human Services web site (http://www.hhs.gov/ocr/privacy/hipaa/administrative/securityrule/securityruleguidance.html), especially the PDF "Security Standards: Implementation for the Small Provider" (http://www.hhs.gov/ocr/privacy/hipaa/administrative/securityrule/smallprovider.pdf).

Start With Yourself

Before you go sign Business Associate Agreements (see Chapter Thirty-One), you need to make sure you are compliant. Assuming you are a pretty normal I.T. consulting company, you don't handle individually identifiable patient health information (patient records) in your office or one your computers, tablets, USB keys, or phones. In other words, there's nothing in YOUR office or possession that is

Copyright © 2014 Karl W. Palachuk

protected information. So documenting your compliance is pretty straight forward.

You need to document how you handle protected information (in paper or electronic format) when you are providing service to the covered entity. Again, in most cases, you "handle" this information only when you are working on client computers or moving data. But you almost never see any actual patient information (hence the term "individually identifiable" patient health information).

So you need a tiny little binder that you can keep in your office. In that binder you need some kind of documentation that shows you have been trained on HIPAA. This could even be self-training by reading official government web sites. But you need to document it.

Next you need a statement about when and where you might have access to individually identifiable patient health information and how you handle such information. Again, this can be a paragraph or two typed up, because you just don't have much exposure.

Finally, you need copies of your Business Associate Agreements that you've signed with all clients.

Everything needs to be dated.

That's it for you. Basically, you need to be able to hand that binder to someone who wants proof of your HIPAA compliance.

Documenting Covered Entities

Covered Entities are a little more complicated because they obviously do have individually identifiable patient health information and access it every day. Remember the three components: training, compliance, and documentation. You'll need a slightly larger binder for your clients.

Copyright © 2014 Karl W. Palachuk

First, you should have a section where you document each employee's training. Whether this was provided by you or someone else. If you hold a company-wide training, you simply need to describe that in a paragraph and list the employees who attended. For on-going training after that, the client will need to make sure this section is kept up to date.

Second, you need two sections on compliance. The first is a section on technical compliance (related to the HITECH Act – Health Information Technology for Economic and Clinical Health Act). The second is for client procedures about how their office operates. Luckily, you (probably) only have to be involved in the first.

HITECH compliance consists of describing how data are handled, encrypted, etc. and how breaches are handled. For small offices this is not complicated. Electronic medical records (EMR) are going to be inside whatever software the client is using to manage their office. You need to describe how this information is stored, managed, and moved. By "describe" I also mean describing what you've put in place to make sure the client is complying with the HITECH Act.

The client's section on compliance has more to do with the daily procedures of the office. This includes physical barriers so that patients cannot hear conversations, view other patients' charts, etc. It also includes copies of forms that might be used, including a patient privacy policy. Information in this section of the binder is outside the authority of the HITECH Act and you can avoid responsibility for it by simply limiting your services to compliance with the HITECH Act.

Third, the binder needs a section on documentation. The binder itself is documentation, of course. But you need more. You need to put all HIPAA related policies, procedures, and documents here. This includes physical descriptions of how data are handled. It also includes copies of all signed Business Associate Agreements.

Copyright © 2014 Karl W. Palachuk

Finally, you should have procedures in place to make sure that employee training is maintained, data handling procedures are followed, and documentation stays up to date. Personnel changes are a key piece of this. When someone new is hired, they need to be trained in company procedures and HIPAA generally. And that needs to be documented in the binder.

It's Just Another Day . . .

Many techs I've talked to are worried about HIPAA and concerned that they won't be able to take on the challenge of helping clients with HIPAA compliance. But don't panic. This is just another in the woods.

The I.T. business is always changing. And it changes fast. If you've been in business five years, you've seen major changes already. And if you've been in business ten or fifteen or more years, the changes have been huge. We all learned the skills that got us where we are. So now we need to learn some new skills.

The biggest challenge seems to be getting doctors and other covered entities to follow the law. Everything else is just an opportunity to expand your services and make more money.

Copyright © 2014 Karl W. Palachuk

3 and 3

Three Take-Aways from This Chapter:

1. Documentation is the single most important piece of HIPAA compliance.

2. Wrap up your training, compliance, and documentation into a service bundle. You get project labor for part of this and ongoing revenue for compliance and documentation.

3. Even though we tend to focus on the current clients, who might not care, there's a blue ocean filled with doctors who are ready to become HIPAA compliant. Go get them!

Three Action Steps for Your Company:

1. _____

_____

2. _____

_____

3. _____

_____

Copyright © 2014 Karl W. Palachuk

Copyright © 2014 Karl W. Palachuk

34

Adding a New Machine to Managed Services

There are two primary reasons that machines are added to a Managed Service contract: 1) The client hires a new employee, or 2) An existing user gets a new computer. But there are all kinds of other reasons that machines show up (someone just wants two computers, client adds a job-specific machine, etc.). You need to make sure that you handle the billing side correctly as well as the technical side.

Note: If you are taking on a new managed service client, then see Chapter Twenty-Three – "Setting Up a New Managed Service Client."

There are three things you need to get right with a new PC setup: Installation, Documentation, and Billing.

Installation

We have tried to get clients to give us as much advance notice as possible when they are hiring a new person or buying a new desktop/laptop for an employee. As with everything else, planned work is more efficient and less expensive than urgent work.

Most of the technical prep work happens before the user sees you. No matter what kind of machine you supply, you'll need to prep it for the client's network. Even if they buy it and you set it up, you still need to do this prep work. As a rule, the technical prep should not be done at

Copyright © 2014 Karl W. Palachuk

the user's desk. It should be done at your office, or at an unused work area at the client office.

Adding a New Machine to Managed Services

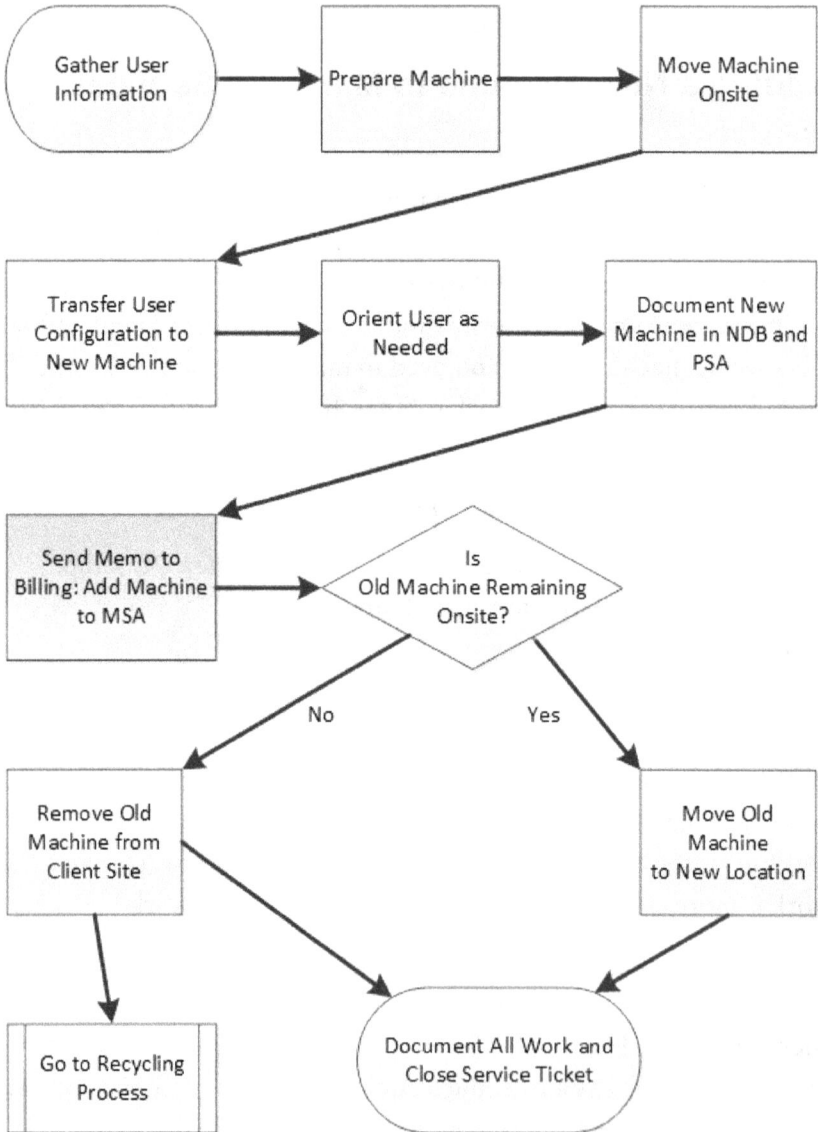

```
  ┌──────────────┐      ┌──────────────┐      ┌──────────────┐
  │ Gather User  │─────▶│   Prepare    │─────▶│ Move Machine │
  │ Information  │      │   Machine    │      │    Onsite    │
  └──────────────┘      └──────────────┘      └──────────────┘

  ┌──────────────┐      ┌──────────────┐      ┌──────────────┐
  │ Transfer User│─────▶│ Orient User  │─────▶│ Document New │
  │Configuration │      │  as Needed   │      │Machine in NDB│
  │to New Machine│      │              │      │   and PSA    │
  └──────────────┘      └──────────────┘      └──────────────┘

  ┌──────────────┐        ◇ Is Old Machine ◇
  │ Send Memo to │─────▶   Remaining Onsite?
  │Billing: Add  │
  │Machine to MSA│        No            Yes
  └──────────────┘

  ┌──────────────┐                      ┌──────────────┐
  │ Remove Old   │                      │   Move Old   │
  │ Machine from │                      │   Machine    │
  │ Client Site  │                      │to New Location│
  └──────────────┘                      └──────────────┘

  ┌──────────────┐      ╭──────────────╮
  │   Go to      │      │Document All  │
  │  Recycling   │      │Work and Close│
  │  Process     │      │Service Ticket│
  └──────────────┘      ╰──────────────╯
```

Copyright © 2014 Karl W. Palachuk

We discuss New PC Checklists in Volume Four of this series. If you do not have a New PC Checklist for this client, now is a good time to start one. If you do have one, make sure you update it before you start and update the master New PC Checklist for that client when you are finished.

Basically, that checklist is going to cover removing trial-ware and junk-ware shipped with the machine, installing client applications, adding hardware drivers as needed, setting up the machine on the domain, and installing your tools for remote monitoring and management (RMM) and professional services administration (PSA). Oh, and moving the user's profile and settings as determined by your policies and any agreements with the client.

While I'm not going into a great deal of detail here, I hope the point is clear: You need good checklists and SOPs to have a pain-free installation of a new machine.

Let's take a quick step back. The reason you need to have checklists and a *rigorous process* is so you can *stay profitable*. Whether you include a new machine setup in your managed service offering or charge for it, you need to complete the job as efficiently as possible. Rework costs money.

If the new machine comes with a new user, you need to make sure they are added as a contact in your PSA (and RMM) system. You will also need to give the new recruit some training on how to create service tickets, what to expect from managed services, and how best to communicate with you.

Copyright © 2014 Karl W. Palachuk

Documentation

In addition to the New PC Checklist, we have two other types of documentation that need to take place. One is the on-site documentation in the Network Documentation Binder (NDB). You need to create a page for the new machine (see *The Network Documentation Workbook*). If you are removing a machine, you'll need to draw a line across the page of the old machine and make a note that it was removed from service.

You will need to make parallel changes in your electronic documentation (PSA and possibly RMM). You need to make sure the new machine is added. If the old machine is being removed, you'll need to remove it from the PSA and RMM services. Some of this is billing related, but most of it is just keeping your documentation clean and up to date so you can rely on it. Yes it takes time. Either add the five minutes to your billing or include it in your calculations for the cost of delivering managed services.

Billing

This is the most important part. After all, this is the part that keeps your lights on! You should have a written policy about your billing with regard to new machines.

First, you need to decide what your policies are around adding new machines. This is obviously something you can bill for one way or another. It is, after all, an "add-move-change" order. We include the first three hours of labor to set up a new machine in our managed service agreement (MSA). And we need to be very clear about this: That means setting up a new machine with a new user. We pay for this by requiring a four-month minimum for any machine added to an MSA.

We do not cover any labor related to replacing an old machine with a new machine for an existing user. We normally cap that at three hours, and it normally takes a lot less. We have a three hour limit because some clients (e.g., accountants) have lots of different software packages that need to be installed.

Second, you need to have a very clear procedure for billing around the addition of machines and the removal of machines. There's one important piece of this that might surprise you. See the illustration.

- When a machine is added to a managed service agreement (MSA), there is a charge equivalent to one month's service on the MSA. For example, if the regular charge is $65/month for a desktop, then that will be the charge at the time the new machine is set up.

We do not sell partial or pro-rated months. Therefore, the charge is $65 no matter when the setup takes place. If the client says it's unfair because it's the 15th, just explain that they're getting three hours of installation labor for that. To be honest, we've had about two questions on this in the last five years.

In Volume One, Chapter Twenty-One we talked about "Invoice Review and Processing." One piece of that is to make sure that all machines added to an MSA are invoiced properly. Another piece is to remove machines when they are no longer being managed.

- When a machine is removed from the client site, you need to have a process for removing that machine from maintenance. This means removing agents you have, recapturing licenses for RMM agents, anti-virus, and any other services you've deployed. All these little things might be $1-5 per month, but unused licenses certainly add up.

You also need to have a system for removing the machine from billing. You ONLY do this when one of your technicians removes that machine from the client site OR the machine has been off and has not reported into the monitoring system for a full billing cycle. When a machine is removed from managed services, the client's monthly bill needs to be adjusted in your PSA.

- Here's the important piece that might surprise you: Some machines never disappear.

From time to time, clients replace an old machine with a new machine. But they re-purpose that old machine. For whatever reason, they just keep using it. Maybe it becomes the official scanning computer. Or the boss decides to put all her graphic files on it. Or whatever.

The point is: That machine continues to report in. It continues to be monitored and patched. It continues to use a license.

And therefore it continues to be on managed services.

That's why our process is to deal with adding a machine completely separately from removing a machine from managed services. First add the new machine. And bill for it. If the old machine goes offline, remove it from billing. In this case there will be two charges for that one user's machines in a single month. This is because we don't pro-rate for partial months and both machines are "on" the service plan for some period of time.

Second, remove that old machine only when it really goes offline. If it never goes offline, you just added a new desktop to the regular billing and no further changes are needed.

In all of this, good communications with your client are important. Good communications within your team is also important. Techs need to have a way to inform the front office when a machine goes on or off managed services.

Copyright © 2014 Karl W. Palachuk

3 and 3

Three Take-Aways from This Chapter:

1. Make sure that technicians are rigorous about your process for adding machines. Lots of money can be lost if this is not executed according to your policies.

2. Agents don't lie. If a machine doesn't disappear, it's still being monitored – and you need to bill for it.

3. You need to set some limits on labor because odd things happen. But you also need to build in processes to make the service fee as flat as possible.

Three Action Steps for Your Company:

1. _____

_____

2. _____

_____

3. _____

_____

Copyright © 2014 Karl W. Palachuk

Copyright © 2014 Karl W. Palachuk

35

How To Use Velcro

Sometimes you need to address the really big issues. This is not one of those times. But this procedure gives you a good idea of the kind of little detail that can make your organization stand out. We cover another example of this in Chapter Thirty-Nine, "Labeling Equipment."

Little things like this truly separate the pros from the newbies. Every profession has "little things" that you learn over time from trial and error – or working with a pro. Clients may never notice the little things. But they will benefit from the little things. And sometimes, as with Velcro, they *will* notice if you do it wrong.

Without further adieu, here's the policy:

SOP: How to Use Velcro

- Overview -

There are many kinds of Velcro products that we might use from time to time. There are two primary uses: 1) Tying cables together, such as cable management on a rack, or 2) Securing equipment to a shelf or wall.

Carrying Velcro Ties is a standard part of the technician's tool kit (see Chapter Twenty-One). Normally, technicians are not required to

Copyright © 2014 Karl W. Palachuk

carry the larger sticky-back Velcro. A little of that is handy, but it's primarily used when setting up equipment. Technicians should always have a roll of Velcro ties.

It is a good habit to do a little clean-up of any cabling you work with. Obviously, anything you are installing fresh should be clean and neat and beautiful. But even when you need to move a few wires on a snake pit of an equipment rack, you should clean it up a bit.

The more important (and less obvious) guidelines for Velcro involve the mounting of equipment.

Rules for Mounting Equipment with Velcro

Velcro has two components – one is scratchy and one is soft. The single most important rule of using Velcro to mount equipment is that you ALWAYS put the soft side on the bottom of the equipment. This does several things for you.

First, if the soft side is on the bottom of the equipment, it cannot scratch shelving or furniture it's placed on. Clients may not appreciate this – but really wouldn't appreciate it if you scratch the hell out of their furniture. And while we normally place routers, switches, and firewalls on equipment racks or crumby shelves in the equipment room, you never know where it might get moved to in the future.

From time to time, you will need to stack some equipment. When you do that, you will always need to have one side of the Velcro on the top and another side on the bottom. Whichever side is on top

Copyright © 2014 Karl W. Palachuk

must always be on top. And whichever side is on the bottom must always be on the bottom. That way, anything can be stacked on anything and you don't have to think about it.

Bring it all together: The same side always has to be on the bottom. It's best to have the soft side on the bottom, so you ALWAYS put the soft side on the bottom of the equipment.

A Note On Wall Mounting Equipment

From time to time you need to mount a device on the wall, normally on plywood in the telephone equipment room. It's a good idea to keep some drywall screws in your tool kit. Sometimes you can put the screws directly into the plywood and mount the device that way.

If you need to (or prefer to) use Velcro, it's obvious which side to mount on the wall, right? The bottom of the equipment will have the soft side, so you need to mount the scratchy side on the wall.

Even the Velcro that's self-stick will probably not stick to plywood for very long. So take those drywall screws and use them to mount the scratchy side of the Velcro.

You need to use the same rule (Always put the soft side on the bottom of the equipment) with wall mounted equipment because you don't know where it might be in the future.

Write up a brief description of the procedure and put it into your SOP binder.

Copyright © 2014 Karl W. Palachuk

3 and 3

Three Take-Aways from This Chapter:

1. Yes, there really is a policy for everything.

2. Always put the soft part of Velcro on the bottom of the equipment.

3. Technicians should carry some Velcro cable ties, but don't normally need the larger rolls of Velcro.

Three Action Steps for Your Company:

1. _____

   _____

2. _____

   _____

3. _____

   _____

36

DNS and DHCP Allocation - Server vs. Firewall

A few years ago, one of the major "truths" about our business changed. It had long been the wisdom that DHCP and DNS should be served from the Windows Server, specifically from the (primary) domain controller. The primary reason for this is that we ("we" being Windows engineers) find it very convenient to manage DHCP from the same place where we manage DNS. But DHCP does not have to be served from the same place as DNS.

Because they're inter-connected, we're going to talk about routers/firewalls, DNS, and DHCP. We'll cover the first two fairly quickly because they are not really up for debate. DHCP is another topic.

Routers and Firewalls

In many documents, Microsoft simply refers to "the router" to describe whatever device you point to to move data off the local area network. Strictly speaking this is a gateway. And for 95% of all the networks we work with, that gateway is a firewall.

There are basically three kinds of firewalls you'll come across: 1) Old, junkie firewalls that are not very configurable; 2) Super powerful firewalls that can absolutely do whatever you want; and 3) Plug and

Play firewalls that can be configured by automated scripts to do what you need them to do.

Most of the arguments in favor of putting DHCP on the server make reference to the first kind of firewall. This has literally become a straw man argument. These firewalls are almost non-existent today. This is particularly true when you consider how little we actually ask the firewall DHCP service to do.

The high-end firewalls can, by definition, do what we need them to do. The only question is whether we choose to use that function.

The third kind of firewall – Universal Plug and Play or UPnP – has evolved relatively recently. UPnP is defined and promoted by the **UPnP Forum**, an industry collaboration that seeks to help manufacturers develop devices that can discover each other and configure automatically. See http://www.upnp.org/. UPnP has been around for most of a decade. It was published as an international standard in 2008 and has been refined considerably since then.

Most consultants have not really paid attention to the evolution of UPnP. You can review the specifications at http://upnp.org/sdcps-and-certification/standards/sdcps/. You will want to look at the specific notes under Internet Gateway:1 and Internet Gateway:2.

One of the cool things that UPnP can do is to understand DNS and become a DNS forwarder. This includes the DNS portion of active directory. Don't get too far ahead of me here, but imagine if the server could automatically configure the UPnP firewall.

DNS Belongs on The Server

This discussion will be short and to the point: Put DNS on the Server. Now, really, you could make the firewall a backup DNS controller

Copyright © 2014 Karl W. Palachuk

and have it get info from the server. But since you're all on the same network, it makes sense to just go to the server.

DNS is critical for directory services. This is particularly true when the server is hosting a variety of functions, such as the old Small Business Servers. "//Companyweb" is not an entry you'll find in a lot of DNS servers. But if you don't have it in your in-house DNS server, you'll need to add it to a hosts file on each machine.

Microsoft pretty much requires the following:

1. Primary DNS is on the Server

2. All workstations point to the server for DNS

We like to add the following two items:

3. The server forwards requests to Google Public DNS (8.8.8.8 and 8.8.4.4) and NOT the ISP

4. Local workstations use the Google Public DNS as their secondary

Number 3 is because ISPs are horrible at keeping clients informed when they change DNS addresses. In addition, this setup means you don't have to change anything if you change ISPs or your ISP changes your IP address.

Number 4 increases the probability that workstations will be able to reach the Internet even if the server is unavailable. The only glitch is when the server is half-up, reachable by ICMP, but the DNS service is not responding. This is a very rare occurrence.

Copyright © 2014 Karl W. Palachuk

DHCP: Server or Firewall?

Without getting into details on some private conversations with people at Microsoft, let me just say that putting DHCP on the server was resulting in many, many calls to tech support. One goal for moving it was simply to create a more stable environment, thus resulting in fewer calls.

A big clue about where the industry standard is going is:

By default, all versions of SBS 2011 and Windows Server 2012 do not enable the DHCP function on the server.

The official recommendation is that DHCP is on the router (firewall).

In fact, these operating systems automatically configure the router with DHCP.

Since SBS 2008, the server has always been able to set up UPnP routers (firewalls). But since the protocol was very new in 2008, I think there was not much noise about it.

See http://blogs.technet.com/b/sbs/archive/2011/09/22/running-dhcp-server-on-sbs-2011-essentials-with-a-static-ip.aspx. And see http://social.technet.microsoft.com/wiki/contents/articles/923.aspx.

Many firewalls also serve up wireless access, and that subnet needs to have its own DHCP. Putting both DHCP scopes on the same device (the firewall) allows that device to manage traffic between the wired and wireless subnets very efficiently.

If you have a plug and play firewall, these Windows Servers will configure the firewall to turn on DHCP, set up the appropriate IP range, and exclude the server's static IP. Note that DHCP will be set up with Dynamic DNS enabled. So both the firewall and the server will exchange information about the devices on the network.

Copyright © 2014 Karl W. Palachuk

On a Standard SBS Server (2011), you have many options that need to be configured. Depending on which options you enable, the UPnP configuration will open only the necessary ports, including

> SMTP - TCP 25
>
> HTTP - TCP 80
>
> HTTPS - TCP 443
>
> SharePoint via RWW - TCP 987
>
> VPN - TCP 1723
>
> RDP - TCP 3389

AND it will forward each of these ports to the Windows Server. So the ports are not just fully open, but can only be used to access the server.

After the server is finished configuring the firewall with UPnP, the Windows Console collects and displays information about your firewall so you can verify it. To see this information, simply view the Internet connection properties.

NOTE: Even if your firewall does not have UPnP enabled, I believe you should put DHCP on the firewall. I only mention the UPnP information to make the point that this is the emerging default. So people with lots of money to spend on research think it's a good idea.

What About VPN?

When I present this information in public, I'm always asked about VPN. Don't you have to enable DHCP on the server in order to use the server for RRAS or VPN?

No.

Copyright © 2014 Karl W. Palachuk

The VPN service (RRAS) hands out IP addresses to anyone who dials in. If you know what you're doing, and have a reason, you can also hard code IP addresses for machines that dial in. But basically, the VPN service has its own little DHCP-like service that hands out addresses and a few scope options (DNS, gateway) to the machine calling in.

If you are suspicious about this, enable the RRAS role but not the DHCP role. You will still be able to connect. In fact, I'll be you have some machines out there that are already configured that way and you just didn't know it.

Advantages of DHCP on the Server?

The primary advantage I hear about having DHCP on the server is that we find it very convenient to manage DHCP from the same place where we manage DNS. (See the first paragraph above.) Okay, that's fine. But think about it. You normally configure DHCP once and never again.

You might make a little change here or there if you migrate a Primary Domain Controller. But having DHCP on the firewall makes that migration a lot easier. As you muck around with DNS settings between the old and new servers, have both servers up at once, and reboot the old and new servers for various reasons, DHCP will simply hum along on the firewall – and no one in the office will know the difference.

Technically, configuring both DHCP and DNS on the same machine might be a bit easier. But since you have to open a new screen for configuring the DHCP role or a new screen for configuring the firewall, it's all the same to me.

Copyright © 2014 Karl W. Palachuk

I believe DHCP is more stable on the firewall and makes the network more stable. The server is infinitely more likely to be rebooted than the firewall.

Implementation

Implementing this policy is really just a matter of making everyone on the support team aware. You might write up a brief memo that says "It is our policy to serve DHCP from the firewall unless there is a specific reason to do otherwise." And then give a brief description of the preferred configuration, similar to what I posted above.

You will need to update any existing checklists and make sure this configuration choice is built into checklists going forward.

Copyright © 2014 Karl W. Palachuk

3 and 3

Three Take-Aways from This Chapter:

1. DNS belongs on your primary server (domain controller).

2. DHCP belongs on the firewall.

3. If you haven't played with UPnP on the newer servers, you should. The protocol works very smoothly these days.

Three Action Steps for Your Company:

1. _____

    _____

2. _____

    _____

3. _____

    _____

Copyright © 2014 Karl W. Palachuk

37

IP Address Allocations

This is definitely more of a technical than a business discussion. But as with most things technical, you can save money and be more efficient if you handle it right.

Most of us inherit whatever IP scheme existed before we showed up. And we pretty much let it go on that way. But as you administer more and more clients, there's a lot of efficiency to be coaxed out of consistency between clients.

In my *Network Documentation Workbook* I have several forms related to the network, and one in particular on IP Address Allocation. Here's some of the Standard Operating Procedure behind that form.

Overview

This is one of those "What happens if you get hit by a bus?" forms. If there's only one person who knows the range of addresses allocated for printers, administration can get expensive.

Of course there are two pieces to the IP Address: The address space and the subnet mask. While firewall vendors and router manufacturers love to push us into the 192.168.1.x address space, there are plenty of other options available. For the official low-down on the private addresses you can use, see these docs: RFC 1918 (The Official, Dry Description of Private IP Addresses) at

Copyright © 2014 Karl W. Palachuk

http://www.ietf.org/rfc/rfc1918.txt or the Microsoft Technet Description of Private IP Addresses at http://technet.microsoft.com/en-us/library/cc958825.aspx.

Given all the options and equipment available today, I recommend a Class C for the client office. In fact, a full Class C (254 addresses). This means your internal network subnet mask is always 255.255.255.0. Remember that you have the following IP address spaces (subnets) available to you:

> 192.168.0.x - 192.168.255.x
>
> 172.16.0.x - 172.31.255.x
>
> 10.0.0.x - 10.255.255.x

The main thing you need to care about with regard to the address space is that **no client should have the same address space as your company**. The reason for this is very simple: You might need to set up a VPN to the client at some point. And if you both have the same subnet (e.g., 192.168.0.x), then your router won't actually route traffic over the VPN because it will think you're on the same subnet (and, therefore, there's no reason to route).

This might be a remote possibility – excuse the pun – but it's worth keeping in mind just in case. And it's pretty easy to do. If you have a 10 or 172 address space, your chances of running into an identical address space are very slim. For example, 10.12.123.x.

After you decide on the IP address space, you need to have a scheme for the last three digits. We use IP allocations something like this (refers to the last quartet of the IP address):

> 1-20 Network Equipment
>
> 26-50 Servers
>
> 76-100 Printers and other connected devices

Copyright © 2014 Karl W. Palachuk

101-200 DHCP for Desktops

201-250 Telephones

Another network/subnet for RAS (personal preference)

Hey, am I trying to pull something? There are gaps here. I like to leave some wiggle room. If I've learned one thing about technology, it's that I can't tell the future. While it seems unlikely that a whole class of devices needing IP addresses will suddenly appear, I have to humbly admit that most networks didn't use TCP/IP at all twenty years ago. And we didn't even have a range for telephones until just a couple years ago.

Implementation Notes

You can easily create this form for your binder. Simply use one column for the range and one column for the description. The actual implementation might take some time.

On **new, fresh networks**, you can simply set your ranges and execute.

On **older, existing networks**, you'll need to phase in execution. It can be disruptive to move printer addresses around, especially if printers are installed with direct printing on each desktop. Servers are also a bit tricky, but less so. Moving their IP address might cause some problems with the NetBIOS name cache. Clearing the cache or simply rebooting machines can take care of this.

But for maximum success, you'll just need to be patient and assign new printers and servers to their new IP ranges. Eventually, the old machines will go away. Having said that, a **network migration** is a great opportunity to implement the new address scheme as you'll

Copyright © 2014 Karl W. Palachuk

have lots of other changes going on, you'll already be scheduled to hit every desktop to make sure everything works, and you might be moving DHCP and DNS services around anyway.

So, whether old or new, you'll gradually move each type of device into the appropriate ranges.

DHCP is its own category, of course. Simply redefine the scope to the new "approved" range. As machines reboot or DHCP leases expire, the new range will simply take care of itself.

Benefits

The biggest benefit of documenting how you use (and will use) IP addresses is that you never have to worry that you'll use an already-assigned IP. This is important for your team, but it's also important when working with other vendors. The most common "other vendor" you'll deal with on this is the dude who installs the big scanner/printer/fax machines.

They tend to run ipconfig/all to find the range and then just randomly assign a number from that range. Sometimes they even assign the wrong subnet mask or (I'm not kidding), serve up DHCP. All of these actions can break the network. Everything breaks except the new printer. So who does the client call? YOU.

It is much better if

1) The client lets you know when the printer dude is coming,

and

2) YOU assign the IP address and tell him what it is.

And that's a perfect example of why this policy is good to have. You simply open the Network Documentation Binder, look at the IP Allocation page, and assign the next available printer address. Zero hassles. Zero guesswork.

This kind of policy requires that everyone on the team

1) Be aware of the policy

2) Practice the policy

3) Correct one another's errors

4) Support one another with reminders

Copyright © 2014 Karl W. Palachuk

3 and 3

Three Take-Aways from This Chapter:

1. The more consistency you build into all of your clients' networks, the more efficient your operation will become.

2. Educate yourself on the options available to you and make intentional choices about your IP Address Allocation policies.

3. Hold a staff training on this and remind technicians of it going forward.

Three Action Steps for Your Company:

1. _____

   _____

2. _____

   _____

3. _____

   _____

Copyright © 2014 Karl W. Palachuk

38

Router and Firewall Configurations

Sometimes, the most important policies and the little, daily routines that can save your bacon in the long run. A great example of this is Router Configurations and Firewall Configurations. Note: I might sometimes use the term "router" by itself. Assume we're talking about routers and firewalls throughout.

Overview

Routers and Firewalls are interesting equipment. They are critical to our success, critical to the client's network, and completely ignored. At least they're ignored when they work perfectly!

If there's any general "problem" with modern routers, it's this: They almost NEVER need attention. But when they do, it's needed urgently. As a rule, we set up routers and firewalls when they're new. They we don't touch them until a specific changed is needed (e.g., mapping at external IP to an internal IP), or the client changes ISPs.

Aside from being competent to configure these devices (not the topic here), you really only have two issues with routers and firewalls:

1) You can't get in because you don't have the logon credentials

2) The configuration gets nuked (by electronics, by accident, by a fool who works for a company other than yours)

Copyright © 2014 Karl W. Palachuk

Luckily, these can be solved with documentation and a couple of very simple SOPs - Standard Operating Procedures.

Documentation Rules!

Okay, let's be honest. One of the most frustrating things about this profession is to come across a router that is totally useless because the previous technician . . .

1) Didn't change the passwords

2) Didn't write down the passwords,

OR

3) Left and won't give you the passwords.

This happens ALL the time. I don't know why these people aren't sued by business owners every day. It's amazing to me. I know they think they're somehow protecting their jobs. But the fact that you're here cracking into their router suggests that they've lost that battle.

Anyway . . . Grrr . . .

We have an easy way of never losing the passwords and logon information to the routers/firewall: **Use your label maker** to put the logon credentials on the bottom of the device. As long as you're at it, label the Router "Router" and label the firewall "Firewall." That will help your clients locate them when you need to walk them through a reboot over the phone.

Some people get in an uproar about putting the password on the bottom of the device. Unless this client ALSO has a web cam connected to a web site, pointed at the bottom of the router, there's no way for someone on the Internet to break into their system just because you put a label on the router. It can't happen.

But what CAN happen is that you get hit by a bus and your client (or another tech) can't get into their own firewall.

The next level of documentation is to fill out the Router or Firewall configuration form (see sample forms in The Network Documentation Workbook). Basically, this form includes logon info, IP addressing, route mapping, access rules, QOS information, etc. The Router or Firewall configuration form goes in the Network Specs section of the Network Documentation Binder.

The final step of documentation is to add this information into your PSA system. We have documentation divided into various categories. Routers and Firewalls go under "hardware" and include a summary of all relevant configuration information. The most important piece of this is the administrator user name and password.

Backup Rules!

Once you have a router/firewall set up – or any time anyone changes anything – you need to back up the configuration. Our standard procedure is this:

- Before you make any changes, back up the router to the c:\!Tech\Hardware\Network directory on the primary server. This is always accessible from the inside network, so it's a perfect place to put it. The file name should be in the format of YYYYMMDDxx, where xx is an increment for the day.

For proper date formats, see Volume Two, Chapter Thirty-One.

- After you make any changes, back up the router to the c:\!Tech\Hardware\Network directory on the primary server. Same file name format.

This before/after routine makes absolutely certain that you can go back to where you were before you touched the device. Yes, according to this procedure there should be a backup already. But you're being very cautious because it takes three minutes and you're a belt-and-suspenders kind of technician!

Note the increments: You might need to make several changes, test them from outside the network, reboot lots of equipment, etc. You may have three or four configurations if you get into a troubleshooting mode. The xx increment is very important. Don't keep backing up over the same file: If something goes wrong you could lose the new and the last version. Slow down, get more done.

Once you're done for the day, you can upload the most recent configuration file to your PSA system as a document. That way, you have just one more backup in case something happens to that server.

Note on file names: You might also append a note to the file name. For example, "2011071502 firewall after new terminal server install.config".

Note on cheap firewalls (routers). If you have a firewall (router) that does not have a tool for backing up the configuration, send an email to your sales manager, asking him to send the client a quote for a real firewall (router).

Copyright © 2014 Karl W. Palachuk

A Couple More Notes

We also have a couple of minor SOPs to make life a little easier with firewalls and routers.

First, we really try to stick with two brand name vendors and only sell business-class equipment. I don't want any clients relying on $40 firewalls and wondering why they're not getting the performance they deserve. I want something with a good warranty, good documentation, and a good reputation with partners.

Second, we configure routers and firewalls so that they can only be configured from inside the network. That means we have to be on site, or we remote into the server and then open the firewall configuration page. Most ISPs require that they can get to your router from the outside, but most lock this down to access from within their network. So that's cool.

We also have policies about IP Address allocation and which we've covered in the previous chapter.

Implementation Notes

You will need a configuration checklist for routers and one for firewalls. You will also need the configuration form discussed.

The checklist and configuration forms should be printed at the same time since you'll go through them together. The checklist will lay out all of the steps we mentioned above as well as specific procedures for your company. You may even have one for each brand (e.g., SonicWall vs. WatchGuard) so you can be very precise in you click-by-click instructions.

When you first start to deploy with this method, you might even put specific instructions in the service ticket. Call out that the tech will back up the configuration, map the IP addresses, change the access rules, save the config, and backup again.

If there has ever been a great argument for why you need a *printed* Network Documentation Binder, it's router configurations. When there's no Internet, or you're between ISPs, then keeping this information on your cloud drive or SharePoint is totally worthless.

Depending on your forms, you might have a little extra space. That's a good place to list out some commonly used port numbers as a reference for your technicians. This is particularly true with SBS and some newer technologies that use non-universal port numbers.

Who Needs To Know?

At the beginning of this article I mentioned that we tend to set up routers (firewalls) and then not touch them for a long time. As a result, you are NOT likely to remember every setting on every router at every client. Documentation is extremely important. Documenting the PROCESS that makes that documentation possible is also critically important.

You probably have one tech who is the "guru" and handles most router/firewall configurations. It doesn't have to be that way, especially with modern equipment, which is pretty easy to configure. Having a good SOP allows you to train other techs very easily.

Copyright © 2014 Karl W. Palachuk

3 and 3

Three Take-Aways from This Chapter:

1. Go a little overboard about backing up router and firewall configurations. It takes a minute and might save you hours.

2. Store the router logon credentials on the bottom of the router. Guaranteed success!

3. Notice that a number of SOPs are beginning to converge in these processes. Naming conventions, IP address allocations, backup habits. It's all one big, profitable system!

Three Action Steps for Your Company:

1. _____

   _____

2. _____

   _____

3. _____

   _____

Copyright © 2014 Karl W. Palachuk

Copyright © 2014 Karl W. Palachuk

39

Labeling Equipment (etc.)

If there's one thing a nerd loves, it's a good label maker!

Of course you can you can get carried away. But you can also do too little. The purpose of labeling is to make your life easier. To the extent that it makes your life easier, you should do it. Here are a few guidelines we use.

Labeling Equipment

As a rule, there are only a few labels we like to see on equipment. After all, you have to admit that labels are not very attractive. The basic guideline is easy: If you are standing in front of a piece of equipment and just need some little bit of information, it should be on a label.

There are two kinds of labels you will use. Some labels are intended for your clients. Others are intended for you and your team. A perfect example of this is with printers. You need to know the IP address and the client needs to know which way to put in letterhead.

I always get a question or two about security, so let me address that up front. For most small and medium businesses, there is very little concern that someone will break into the network from the inside, reconfigure printers, etc. You need to be prudent, but don't get carried away.

Copyright © 2014 Karl W. Palachuk

At the same time, small and medium businesses have a never-ending problem of poor documentation. So very often you don't have the most basic information you need in a handy little binder next to the server. How many times have you taken on a new client who has no login credentials for their router? Or (for whatever reason) there is a password on the printer's configuration web server. Sometimes you can "fix" this by resetting the equipment to factory specs, but that often means you don't have the configuration information you need.

For example, I firmly believe that the login username and password should be labeled on the bottom of firewalls and routers. That scares some people because it is such a critically important piece of the network's security. This is not a security issue for one simple reason: No one from the Internet can see the bottom of the firewall! This is a matter of physical (access) security, not network security.

But on the day you need to get into that router, it's very handy to know that you can turn it over and get the information you need! I've come across dozens of routers and firewalls with no documentation. In twenty years, I was able to figure out (guess) the password on exactly one router.

Now let's look at specific equipment.

Firewalls and Routers:

1) Place a label on the front/top of the router that simply says "Router" in very large type. Place a label on the front/top of the firewall that simply says "Firewall" in very large type. This is very handy when you're on the phone with the client and you are walking them through some troubleshooting, such as power cycling the right piece of equipment or reporting which lights are on.

2) Place a label on the back/bottom of routers and firewalls with the login username and password. As long as you're printing out this label, make an extra copy to put on the configuration page for your Network Documentation Binder. You might also label the LAN and WAN IP addresses, although that information is very easy to discover by other means if you need it.

3) More than any other equipment, it is critical that you update the label with new login information when it changes! The only thing worse than having no login info is having the wrong info!

Switches:

Unless you have managed switches, you probably don't need to label switches. If you think you might need to talk the client through some troubleshooting by phone, you might put a label on the front that just says "Switch."

For managed switches, you should use the same labeling procedure as you have for firewalls and routers.

Network Printers and Scanners:

1) Each network printer should have a label with its name clearly visible on the front. This is handy for you and the client.

2) Each network printer should have a label with its IP address (and each printer should have a static IP). This can go on the back or maybe inside a panel that opens.

3) If a printer is ever used for printing checks, envelopes, or letterhead, it is VERY handy to have a label that gives the user a clue about how to place specialty paper for printing. For example, "Face Up; Top Out." Yes, I know there's probably one of those

Copyright © 2014 Karl W. Palachuk

little icons with the front or back indicator, but many clients don't see those icons, or don't understand them. Why not make their life a little easier?

Servers:

1) You might have a label on the server that says "Server" or has the server name. But unless you have two servers and the client needs to know which is which, this is completely optional.

2) Instructive labels on the back side of the server are frequently very handy. For example, if you have an ILO (Integrated Lights Out) or DRAC (Dell Remote Access Controller) port, a good clear label for that is useful. This is particularly true if you un-plug the cable from the ILO/DRAC port for whatever reason.

   Sometimes it is helpful to place a "Do not use" label across an unused NIC port so that no one plugs a cable in there and causes havoc with the network. And with some clients it's useful to put a "Do not use" label across a modem port so no one plugs anything into that.

3) Inside the computer, you should label each hard drive. This is true whether they are hot-swappable or not. All you need to put on the drive is Drive 0, Drive 1, Drive 3, etc. You may choose to label drives with Drive C, Drive D, etc. if that's useful. But the main goal of labeling drives is so you can use the labels for troubleshooting in the future.

   This may be the most important set of labels you use. When you are troubleshooting RAID controllers or hard drives for any reason, you may find it useful to swap out drives. Knowing the exact configuration before you start troubleshooting can save you many hours of labor. It is also very helpful when you get an alert about drive errors or imminent failure. You can order a replacement drive, but when you hand it to the technician to install, he needs to know which slot to put it into.

Two maxims for successful troubleshooting come into play here. The first is "Know what you know." With properly labeled drives you can feel confident about the order the drives were in when you started. You can keep track of the order in which you tried various configurations while troubleshooting. The second maxim is "Slow down, get more done." While troubleshooting anything, proper labels will allow you to be completely confident about what you've tried already so you do not continually try the same thing over and over again.

4) Finally, you might have labels for other things that are helpful to your techs or your client. For example, if you have more than one power supply, you might label them. Again, while troubleshooting by telephone you can instruct the client to remove PS1 or PS2. Another example is with backup systems. On rare occasions a client might have more than one tape drive or more than one external disc system. With swappable backup hard drives, life is much easier if everything is labeled.

Desktop Computers:

1) Every computer should be labeled with its name. Whether you name machines something boring such as "Workstation 1" or more personalized such as rock stars, cities, car parts, etc., all machines should be labeled. This name should be on the front of the machine and easily visible to users and technicians. While you are making these labels, go ahead and print an extra one to put on the Machine Spec Sheet in your Network Documentation

Copyright © 2014 Karl W. Palachuk

Workbook. (See Chapter Two: "Naming Conventions for Machines and Servers.")

2) If some machines are owned by you as part of a HaaS (hardware as a service) program, they should be clearly labeled with a "Property of ..." label. Similarly, you might label machines that need to be identified as part of a leasing program or machines purchased through a specific funding source for non-profits.

Miscellaneous Equipment:

1) Modems, if you still have such a thing, might be labeled with their associated phone number

2) Print servers should be labeled with their IP address, and possibly other access information

3) In general, think about what happens if equip is unplugged, thrown into a box, and forgotten for six months. When you dig it out and don't have any paperwork, what key information do you need? Label the equipment with that information!

Portable Equipment:

If the client has equipment that goes out in the field, goes home, or goes back and forth between offices, it is probably useful to label this equipment for various reasons. Most of these labels are related to what the equipment is and where it lives. Some equipment needs identifying information or labels that tell when it was new or when it was last serviced.

Copyright © 2014 Karl W. Palachuk

Property Labels:

Lots of things need "Property of ..." labels. This is particularly true of HaaS equipment. But it is also true of any equipment that is ever intended to leave the office for any reason. Also, if you loan equipment to a client, it should be labeled as yours.

Implementation

Implementing this policy is really just a matter of making everyone on the support team aware. You might write up a brief memo that summarizes your policies. Then you need two things: Label makers and checklists. Every technician should carry a label maker in their scary box (see Chapter Twenty-One). Taking this with them to every client visit is simply part of the job.

This policy is most commonly implemented by including instructions in checklists. When you build a machine, the checklist should include instructions for labeling. When you configure a firewall, the checklist should include instructions for labeling. And so forth.

The other common way that this policy is implemented is with service tickets. So, if you don't have a checklist to set up a simple printer, for example, the ticket should specifically list labeling the printer as an item in the ticket. This requires that the service manager be mindful and remember to add that action to the ticket. This amounts to habit, habit, habit.

Copyright © 2014 Karl W. Palachuk

3 and 3

Three Take-Aways from This Chapter:

1. Define these policies for the way *your* company works. Start making them part of your process.

2. If you standardize on a reasonably-priced and widely-available label, you can always buy the same labels, and just make sure each technician has a label maker to match.

3. Label makers take batteries. So you'll want to hit Costco or Sam's Club and stock up on AA batteries.

Three Action Steps for Your Company:

1. _____

   _____

2. _____

   _____

3. _____

   _____

Copyright © 2014 Karl W. Palachuk

40

Removing Old Information - From Everything

Data Data Everywhere

Everyone is aware that you need to protect data on hard drives, and that you need to totally delete that data when drives are taken out of service. There is a very high probability that you have a standard process within your company for disposing of drives, doing secure wipes, etc.

Make sure that you write down that policy and train your techs.

But wait . . . there's more.

We put our hands on all kinds of client data all the time. Usually it's electronic and on the client's machines, so we don't really have to do anything with it. But sometimes we end up with information on paper, such as employee names, computers, IP address schemes, etc. Plus all kinds of documentation in paper format.

And, of course, we have lots and lots of client information in our PSA system (that is, in electronic format on our systems).

In Volume Two, Chapter Thirty-Nine, we talked about shredding policies. In Chapter Twenty-Five of this volume we talked about handling data when a client's employee leaves. Now let's take a broader view of client data that is found at *your* office.

Copyright © 2014 Karl W. Palachuk

Three Kinds of Client Data

In general, you will have client information in three primary places within your possession:

1) Client Files

- With a copy of their contract, important communications, and possibly financial information such as credit card info or cancelled checks

2) Hardware you've removed from the client

- Such as routers, desktop PCs, laptops, servers. Here we're talking about more than just the hard drives.

3) Internal forms and files that you use to support the client

- This includes New PC checklists, Monthly maintenance checklists, printouts you used to complete a task, copies of old Network Migration Binders, etc.

For Client files, you just need a very short policy statement. It should cover who has access to these files, what goes in the files, and what gets "clean out" from files. Something along these lines:

> "Client files will be stored only in the locked file cabinet in _____'s office. All files will be replaced where they belong in the file cabinet when not in use. So, for example, files will not be left out on a desk overnight.
>
> Only _____, _____, and _____ are authorized to access client files at any time.
>
> Client files will include a copy of the most recent service agreement, any important correspondence, and current credit card information IF it is necessary to maintain CC info AND

Copyright © 2014 Karl W. Palachuk

retaining this information in paper format is approved by the client.

Once credit card information is entered into the auto-billing service, it is our policy to shred all copies of this information we possess.

At the end of each calendar year, all client folders are moved to storage in a paper file box labeled with the year. The only information brought forward to the new year is the most recent service agreement."

Client Hardware

Hardware is an interesting information item. In the last chapter we talked about labeling things. Well ... there's an end-game associated with the habit of labeling everything. If you are super good at creating random passwords and never re-using them, then it doesn't matter if the router has the password taped to the bottom.

But clients tend to be horrible at good passwords. Even if they have a good password, they re-use it all the time. To be honest, I do this a lot too. Those 900 web sites I'm registered on? Yeah. Maybe three passwords covers 895 of them. I'm much more secure with the password for payroll processing.

Anyway, clients follow your example. So you label a machine with its name and they add a label for the administrator password. You might even label the local admin password on the back of the machine (after all, no one can see this on the Internet).

So when it's time for recycling that machine, you need to make sure you have a policy to scour all devices for labels and remove them. No matter how innocuous the information is, just get in the habit of removing all these labels.

Copyright © 2014 Karl W. Palachuk

Add that little step to your machine recycling checklist.

Client Information on Your Internal Systems

Finally, we get to internal forms and files that you use to support the client. On the administration and sales side, you will have client roadmap questionnaires and all kinds of information you might have collected or created regarding sales and configurations.

On the technical side you'll have various client-specific checklists, project papers, etc. We keep a copy of every network migration project forever. We actually have a file cabinet in the tech area with big fat pouch files for each migration project. Naturally, this includes all kinds of information about the client's configuration. That data is probably more important than a credit card number.

That's a unique example of sensitive data on the tech side. For the most part, sensitive client information on the tech side is stored in the PSA. But we do print things out, mark them up, and use them for various things. It is extremely important that everyone be in the habit of treating this information with respect.

In our case, some of this information is stored in the brown file cabinet with the migration projects. For example, we have checklists to make sure that backups are checked daily and that monthly maintenances are completed. These are not particularly sensitive data. Actually, they often simply amount to a list of client names. But that's important data.

So on the tech side, we have processes for filing items in the brown file cabinet. Everything else that has client information is covered by the company-wide policy about handling client data. Our company policy about handling client data is very simple:

Copyright © 2014 Karl W. Palachuk

"Some client information in paper format is needed by the front office for finances and client management. All such information will be stored in client folders in a locked file cabinet in the office.

Some client information in paper format is used by the sales department. Because virtually all of this information is saved electronically, it is our policy to shred any paper with any information as soon as that paper is no longer needed. If the sales department wishes to keep documents for long-term storage, they should be given to the office manager to store in the client folder.

Some client information in paper format is used by the tech department and stored long term. All such information must be stored in the brown file cabinet, which should be locked at the end of every day.

Other client information that the tech department has in paper format must be shredded as soon as that paper is no longer needed."

I know this sounds like it's a whole layer of hassle on top of what everyone is already doing, but it's not. First, get over the belief that something has to stay around just because someone printed it. Use it and shred it. Everyone. Every department. Every job. Every day.

If you need to keep something to prove that a job was completed, fine. Figure out where it goes and put it there. But be brutally honest (and remember that 99% of the paper you touch will never be looked at again). If you have something that's not in electronic format (such as a printout from the ISP that the client has written passwords on so you can do an email migration), scan it to PDF and put it in the PSA. Then shred the paper.

Copyright © 2014 Karl W. Palachuk

If you don't want to have a shredder at every desk, that's understandable. Have a centralized shredder or a box for shredding that lives in the office (which is locked at night).

Note on long-term storage: Pick a timeframe and shred those paper file boxes when they get old. For us, all information more than seven years old is shredded. Period. I used to have my daughter do this. Now I take it to the UPS store. It costs me about $25/box. But I was paying my daughter $10/hr. I think UPS is cheaper - and I don't have to buy a new shredder every year.

Note on non-paper stuff: You might also have client information in the form of CD, DVDs, tapes, or even hard drives. You need a process for destroying all of these.

Make Data Destruction Fun

A few years ago we had a client who wanted proof that we had destroyed his old firewall, even though that firewall did not contain logs or other sensitive data. It did, after all, have his internal IP address range and the port mappings for his servers. So even though we can nuke it back to factory specs, some CIA-level tools could probably retrieve the old data.

So we made this video to prove to him that we had destroyed his firewall:

https://www.youtube.com/watch?v=rg_gaYWL8LE

Hey, why not have fun since you have to work anyway?

Copyright © 2014 Karl W. Palachuk

3 and 3

Three Take-Aways from This Chapter:

1. Scour old equipment to remove all labels placed there by your company or the client.

2. Treat all client-identifying data as if it were a credit card number. Shred it. Destroy it. Or keep it under secure lock and key.

3. Do not let technicians pile up paperwork on their desks or in drawers. Invariably, sensitive client data gets piled with the rest.

Three Action Steps for Your Company:

1. _____

   _____

2. _____

   _____

3. _____

   _____

Copyright © 2014 Karl W. Palachuk

Copyright © 2014 Karl W. Palachuk

41

Responding to Viruses

Ugh. We all hate viruses. They represent that rare I.T. problem that can be challenging but not rewarding. When you conquer most problems, you emerge with a better system, a faster network, more storage, . . . or something worthwhile. When you conquer a virus, you just get to use your computer again.

Modern viruses (worms, trojans, etc.) can be almost unbelievably destructive. They can infect every pore of a system – DLL's, registry, operating system files. Everything.

And more importantly, modern viruses can take HUGE amounts of time to fix. And sometimes they can't be fixed. And that means they can be extremely unprofitable! When a new computer with a fast processor and all the software you need is less than $1,500, there's a limit to how many hours you want to spend "fixing" viruses.

A standard operating procedure is in order.

SOP Friday: Responding to Viruses

Overview

Unlike the SOPs we've discussed so far, this one is strictly defensive in nature. How do you restore the machine, keep the client happy,

Copyright © 2014 Karl W. Palachuk

provide a timely response, and make money (or at least not lose money)?

More than anything, virus protection is most successful when you are **very well prepared**. That means the right hardware, the right software, the right configurations, the right customer training, and the right practices. All of that makes it possible for you to have the right response. Without adequate preparation, there may be no good response. Let's divide this world of preparation so we can conquer it.

First, you need to lay the groundwork with **hardware and software**. If you're a managed service provider, your life gets pretty easy here. If you're not, then you just have to convince your clients.

Note: Some of these "policies" are really the essence of Standard Operating Procedures. We recommend one way of doing things. We push. We cajole. We quote the right tools, etc. We can't force a client to protect their systems. Which leads to one of my favorite sayings:

"We can't care more about the client's network than they do."

Our managed services contract (see the book *Service Agreements for SMB Consultants*) specifically requires that the client have a good, working firewall that's **under warranty** or covered by a **maintenance agreement**. In other words, it's the latest and greatest, and can protect them from new attacks that show up unannounced.

It's amazing how effective hardware firewalls can be at detecting and stopping viruses – even the ones where clients are tricked into "installing" the Anti-Virus 2011 (or whatever) virus. Now, let's be

Copyright © 2014 Karl W. Palachuk

honest. We're talking about a $750 firewall, NOT a $49 firewall. See Chapter Thirty-Eight.

As for software . . .

This has two components. First, there's anti-virus software. This one is fairly obvious and takes very little convincing. The main decision is whether you're supplying and annual renewal or a monthly subscription. If you have annual renewals, you need ticklers to remind you to send the invoices.

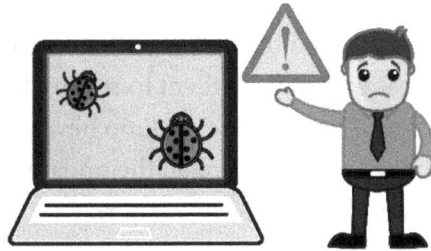

The other piece of the software puzzle is **Newer Programs.** Old programs – such as Microsoft Office 97 and Windows XP have some vulnerabilities that will never be fixed. Newer programs and operating systems are inherently more secure. Moving clients to the newer stuff is a never ending battle. We are constantly reminding clients that modern software is part of their security.

Hardware, operating systems, and software, must all be kept **patched and updated.** That means you need to have those processes as part of your maintenance plan, whether on managed services or not.

Imaging Machines

We do not currently image desktop machines. Our policy is that machines should be properly maintained, we limit our exposure to virus incidents, and we fix machines when a virus hits.

On related notes, it is our policy that we do NOT redirect My Documents to the server. We don't encourage clients to use My Docs. All information that's important needs to live on the server. Period.

Copyright © 2014 Karl W. Palachuk

The server is on redundant drives and backed up. The desktops are essentially disposable.

Having said that, I have often heard people say that they image desktops and use them to restore from virus attacks. This sounds great as long as the desktop never changes. If you need to restore an image and then run all the updates since the image was refreshed, it may not save you any labor.

Imaging is a viable option. We just don't happen to practice it.

Note: We DO allocate space to let Windows store previous versions so we can roll back to before the Virus hit. That has saved our bacon more than one. Just remember to do it.

Client Education

There are two kinds of client education related to viruses. First, there's education on your contract/agreement and what your response will be. Second, there's training on how to avoid viruses and what to do when one hits.

Our contact is very clear on this point: All maintenance, including all software installations, must be performed by an employee of KPEnterprises. So, when a client installs a virus on their computer, it is not covered by the managed services agreement.

Now, the truth is, we're going to believe the client that it's an accident and fix the first incident for free. But we're also going to make it very clear that they next one is on THEM. They'll get a bill for X hours at $00.00/hour. But we'll also make sure they know the next one will be for $150/hour.

Client education consists of emails, memos, newsletters, harping, haranguing, and whatever else we need to get across a few simple points:

1) You already have an anti-virus program. You don't ever need to install another one, no matter what pops up in front of you.

2) Whenever you receive an email with an attachment and you did not ask that person to send you that attachment, Delete It! Period. I don't care if it's your mother or your boss. If need be, email them back and ask if they sent it.

3) Whenever you receive email with links that look urgent, do not click on them. Go to the appropriate web site yourself by typing the regular address into your browser (e.g., your bank). Log in. If there's an urgent matter that needs your attention, it should be flashing in front of your face. Delete the email.

4) If you're browsing the web and a window opens up by itself, click the Red X in the upper right hand corner. Do not click . . .

   - Yes

   - No

   - Accept

   - Decline

   - Close

   - Unsubscribe

   or anything else. Just click the Red X to close the window. If you feel violated, reboot your computer.

5) If you get an infection, log off of your computer. If you can't log off, restart the computer (force a power down and restart) and do NOT log on. We need the computer on to connect remotely.

Copyright © 2014 Karl W. Palachuk

The Bottom Line: Educating your client about your policies and their expected behavior will help limit your liability/exposure during a virus infestation.

Stand Firm by your processes and procedures. 99% of modern viruses are stopped by almost any anti-virus software . . . until the user clicks OK. In other words, it is almost always the user doing this to themselves. They need to understand that.

Standardized Response

So . . . when you finally get a service ticket about a virus infection, what do you do? Here's a rough outline of our process.

1) As with any ticket, determine the urgency and assign a priority level

2) Have a discussion with the client. Remind them about the policies. Verify the maximum number of hours we will put into fixing a machine before we move to billable labor. Request how many hours of billable labor are acceptable before the client wants us to stop working on the issue and simply re-install the O.S.

    It is very important that you agree on limits to your time and to what happens when you reach those limits.

3) Connect to the machine remotely and log on in safe mode.

    We do this with our RMM. If you don't have such remote access, then you'll need to be onsite. In either case, log on in safe mode. This will stop user-specific viruses from continuing to cripple the machine.

Copyright © 2014 Karl W. Palachuk

4) Attempt to clean the machine with your standard company-approved tools. These may include Trend, Symantec, AVG, Hit Man Pro, or whatever your decides is the best fit for you.

5) If #4 appears to work, reboot the machine, log on as the user, and attempt to verify that the virus is gone.

6) If #4 appears not to work, attempt to restore the machine to an earlier version running the tools built into the operating system. If you know the day the machine was infected, you should be able to restore to a previously working version.

7) If you believe the virus has been cleaned, apply all appropriate updates, and create a new restore point.

Implementation Notes

Implementing this policy can be very troublesome. Many clients insist that local users have admin rights. That's not always in their best interest. If you're losing money every time they get a virus, then it's not in your best interest either.

If a client allows themselves to be infected more than once, you really need to take them out of the local administrator's group. This might mean that the client needs to pay you to install a few programs here and there, but the cost is very small compared to a four-hour bill for fixing viruses.

As I mentioned earlier, an appropriate response means the right hardware, the right software, the right configurations, the right customer training, and the right practices. That means you need to really think through these processes and push them on to employees and clients **every time** there's a virus.

Copyright © 2014 Karl W. Palachuk

Note on "All You Can Eat"

I have never been a fan of "All you can eat" managed services. After twenty years in this business, I know "all" some clients can eat is my entire company! Fighting viruses is a perfect example of that. You need to limit your losses with good processes and policies.

Forms

There are no specific forms for implementing this SOP. You might write up a brief description of the procedure and put it into your SOP or binder.

This kind of policy requires that everyone on the team

1) Be aware of the policy

2) Practice the policy

3) Correct one another's errors

4) Support one another with reminders

Copyright © 2014 Karl W. Palachuk

3 and 3

Three Take-Aways from This Chapter:

1. You need good response policies in place before a client reports a virus. You should have consistent policies will all clients.

2. Be careful – and intentional – about how viruses are addressed in your contracts. No matter how you look at it, you are providing a service and deserve to make money on it.

3. With each client, set time limits on trying to fix viruses and determine what happens when you reach the limits.

Three Action Steps for Your Company:

1. _____

   _____

2. _____

   _____

3. _____

   _____

Appendix A:
Definitions and Acronyms

Business Associate Agreement   A contract between covered entities and business associates to ensure that the business associates will appropriately safeguard protected health information. See http://www.hhs.gov/ocr/privacy/hipaa/understanding/coveredentities/contractprov.html for more information.

Checklist   The name given to the finest level of detail for executing the action steps needed to achieve a result. A procedure should include at least one checklist, but might include more than one checklist.

DRAC   Dell Remote Access Controller. See also HP's ILO.

HaaS   Hardware as a Service. Any scheme in while you supply hardware to client for a monthly recurring fee rather than selling them the hardware to them.

HIPAA   The Health Insurance Portability and Accountability Act.

Copyright © 2014 Karl W. Palachuk

HITECH Act The Health Information Technology for Economic and Clinical Health Act. Part of the enforcement rules for HIPAA.

ILO HP's Integrated Lights Out controller. See also Dell's DRAC.

ISO Open Systems Interconnection – a model for describing network connectivity and operations.

MSA Managed Service Agreement

NDB Network Documentation Binder

Process The name given to a series of tasks that result in a general outcome. A process might include several different procedures.

Procedure The name given to a specific set of action steps that achieve an outcome.

PSA Professional Services Administration. A type of software that includes modules for running your professional service business.

RMM Remote Monitoring and Management

SBS Small Business Server

SMB Small and Medium Business

SOP Standard Operating Procedures

TSR Log Troubleshooting and Repair Logs.

UPnP Universal Plug and Play. A protocol for automating the configuration of firewalls and routers.

Copyright © 2014 Karl W. Palachuk

Appendix B: Resources

Articles

Internet Growth 1981-1991. RFC 1296. RFC 1296. See
http://tools.ietf.org/html/rfc1296.

HIPAA Privacy Rule at the Federal Registry:
http://www.gpo.gov/fdsys/pkg/FR-2013-01-25/pdf/2013-01073.pdf

(HIPAA) *Security Standards: Implementation for the Small Provider* –
http://www.hhs.gov/ocr/privacy/hipaa/administrative/securityrule/smallprovider.pdf

Public and Private Addresses – Microsoft Technet Description of Private IP Addresses. http://technet.microsoft.com/en-us/library/cc958825.aspx.

RFC 1918 – The Official, Dry Description of Private IP Addresses. http://www.ietf.org/rfc/rfc1918.txt

Running DHCP Server on SBS 2011 Essentials With a Static IP.
http://blogs.technet.com/b/sbs/archive/2011/09/22/running-dhcp-server-on-sbs-2011-essentials-with-a-static-ip.aspx

Windows Small Business Server 2008: Router Setup.
http://social.technet.microsoft.com/wiki/contents/articles/923.aspx

Copyright © 2014 Karl W. Palachuk

Theodore Woodward biography. Source of the quote "When you hear hoof beats behind you, don't expect to see a zebra." http://en.wikipedia.org/wiki/Theodore_Woodward

Books

The E-Myth Revisited by Michael E. Gerber.

First Things First by Stephen R. Covey, A. Roger Merrill, and Rebecca R. Merrill.

Managed Services in a Month by Karl W. Palachuk.

The Network Documentation Workbook by Karl W. Palachuk. www.networkdocumentationworkbook.com

The Network Migration Workbook by Karl W. Palachuk and Manuel L. Palachuk. www.networkmigrationworkbook.com.

The Power of Focus by Jack Canfield.

Project Management in Small Business by Dana Goulston, PMP, and Karl W. Palachuk.

Relax Focus Succeed by Karl W. Palachuk. www.relaxfocussucceed.com.

Service Agreements for SMB Consultants by Karl W. Palachuk. www.serviceagreementsforsmbconsultants.com.

Software and Services

Autotask. www.autotask.com. One of the most successful PSA systems.

Belarc Advisor. See http://www.belarc.com. Tool for auditing computer configurations.

Copyright © 2014 Karl W. Palachuk

ConnectWise PSA. See www.connectwise.com. One of the most successful PSA systems.

EventID.net. Search by Windows Event ID. www.eventid.net.

Google Alerts. www.google.com/alerts. Receive email "alerts" whenever Google indexes something related to your topic. Good for seeing what others are seeing about your company – or to do your own trickle research.

Robocopy is a tool distributed primarily via the Microsoft Server Resource Kits since NT 3.5. http://technet.microsoft.com/en-us/library/cc733145.aspx.

Tigerpaw Software. See www.tigerpawsoftware.com. One of the most successful PSA systems.

Misc. Web Sites

4Med HIPAA Training – http://www.4medapproved.com.

Belarc Advisor – www.belarc.com.

Firewall Destruction by UHaul (video).
https://www.youtube.com/watch?v=rg_gaYWL8LE

Health and Human Services HIPAA web site –
http://www.hhs.gov/ocr/privacy/hipaa/administrative/securit
yrule/securityruleguidance.html

HIPAA Administration and Information –
www.hhs.gov/ocr/privacy/hipaa/administrative/index.html

HIPAA Pinterest Board – by Karl. Okay to send clients here –
http://pinterest.com/karlpalachuk/hipaa-news/

Lists of Names – A web site with lists of names –
http://listofnames.info

Copyright © 2014 Karl W. Palachuk

Microsoft Security Center – Monthly security bulletin. http://technet.microsoft.com/en-au/security/bulletin/

Small Biz Thoughts blog –http://blog.smallbizthoughts.com.

SMBBooks.com – The primary book store for Karl's books. Also the place where you can register this book to access downloadable content.

Tech Soup – http://www.techsoup.org – Source for non-profit organizations to get software at **extremely** low prices.

UPnP Forum – An industry collaboration that seeks to help manufacturers develop devices that can discover each other and configure automatically – http://www.upnp.org/.

UPnP Specifications – http://upnp.org/sdcps-and-certification/standards/sdcps/.

U.S. Department of Labor – U.S. Fair Labor Standards Act – www.dol.gov/compliance/laws/comp-flsa.htm.

Windows NT 4.0 Post-Service Pack 6a Security Rollup Package (SRP) – http://support.microsoft.com/kb/299444 – I can't imagine you need this, but I mentioned it in the book, so it's in the Resources section.

Copyright © 2014 Karl W. Palachuk

Other Resources from Small Biz Thoughts

Please Check Out Our Web Sites:

www.SMBBooks.com

This is our primary site for books on technical topics, managed services, running your business, and more. All of our up-coming training events and recorded programs are there as well.

www.SmallBizThoughts.com

blog.SmallBizThoughts.com

This is our primary web site and Karl's popular blog for I.T. Consultants and Managed Service Providers. You can also find out about SOPs (standard operating procedures) and business coaching through this web site.

Karl's Weekly Newsletter

Register at one of the sites above or at GreatLittleBook.com.

This newsletter covers upcoming events, seminars, news, and "what's happening" in the SMB Consulting space.

Copyright © 2014 Karl W. Palachuk

Please also consider these fine books by Great Little Book:

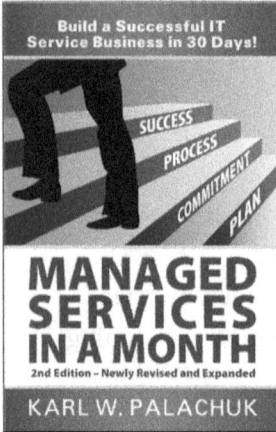

Managed Services in a Month 2nd ed.

Build a Successful IT Services Business in 30 Days.

by Karl W. Palachuk

2013

208 pages

A no-nonsense guide to building a successful managed service practice.

Whether you are just starting out, or converting your existing break/fix technology consulting business to managed services, this book will show you the way. The newly revised and expanded 2nd edition has nine new chapters, covering the latest products and services available today-including cloud technologies.

Also available as an e-book, audio book, or in a Spanish language translation.

The #1 book on Managed Services on Amazon.com for more than five years!

Copyright © 2014 Karl W. Palachuk

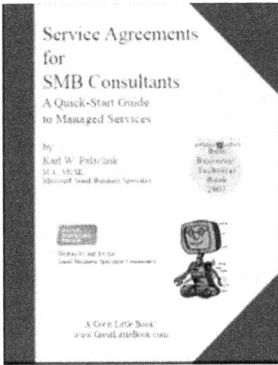

Service Agreements for SMB Consultants

A Quick-Start Guide to Managed Services

by Karl W. Palachuk

2006

185 pages

This great little book does a lot more than give you sample agreements.

Karl starts out with a discussion of how you run your business and the kinds of clients you want to have. The combination of these – defining yourself and defining your clients – is the basis for your service agreements.

Includes sample contracts with commentaries. All text, as well as some other great resources are provided as downloads.

Available in paperback or e-book formats.

www.SMBBooks.com

www.SmallBizThoughts.com

Copyright © 2014 Karl W. Palachuk

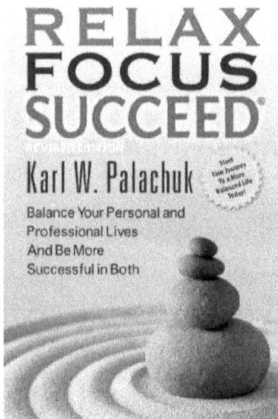

Relax Focus Succeed[®]

Balance Your Personal and Professional Lives and Be More Successful in Both

by Karl W. Palachuk

2013

296 pages

The premise of this book is simple but powerful: The fundamental keys to success are focus, hard work, and balance. Too often, the advice we receive gives plenty of attention to focus and hard work, but very little to balance.

This great little book will help you believe that you need balance, show you the power of focus, and help you move forward with the new you -- a happier, healthier, better balanced, and more successful you.

www.SMBBooks.com

www.SmallBizThoughts.com

Copyright © 2014 Karl W. Palachuk

Copyright © 2014 Karl W. Palachuk

Calling all SMB IT Professionals!

The ChannelPro Network is dedicated to providing IT consultants, VARs and MSPs the news, insights, resources and best practices necessary to help them grow their businesses and better serve their SMB customers.

Sign up for free today
Website | Live Events | Monthly Magazine

ChannelProNetwork.com

www.ingramcontent.com/pod-product-compliance
Lightning Source LLC
Chambersburg PA
CBHW060808220326
41598CB00022B/2567

* 9 7 8 0 9 9 0 5 9 2 3 4 1 *